Every Child a Storyteller

EVERY CHILD A STORYTELLER
A Handbook of Ideas

Harriet R. Kinghorn
and
Mary Helen Pelton

Illustrated by Myke Knutson

1991
TEACHER IDEAS PRESS
A Division of
Libraries Unlimited, Inc.
Englewood, Colorado

TEACHER IDEAS PRESS
A Division of Libraries Unlimited, Inc.
P.O. Box 6633
Englewood, CO 80155-6633
1-800-237-6124

Library of Congress Cataloging-in-Publication Data

Kinghorn, Harriet R., 1933-
    Every child a storyteller : a handbook of ideas / Harriet R.
Kinghorn and Mary Helen Pelton ; illustrated by Myke Knutson.
    xiii, 211 p. 22x28 cm.
    Includes bibliographical references and index.
    ISBN 0-87287-868-6
    1. Storytelling. 2. Storytelling ability in children.
3. Creative activities and seat work. 4. Activity programs in
education. I. Pelton, Mary Helen White. II. Title. III. Title:
Every child a story teller.
LB1042.K53 1991
808.5'43--dc20   91-2709
                                    CIP

We would like to dedicate this book to our friends and husbands, Ray Pelton and the late Norton Kinghorn, for their patience, good humor, and understanding during the time we worked on the manuscript.

Contents

Preface

Human beings are the storytelling animals. What makes us different from other creatures is not our opposable thumbs, not our ability to perambulate on only two legs, not our lack of feathers, but our penchant for creating and using narratives for just about every purpose. We tell stories to entertain ourselves and each other; old people tell stories to young people about the way it used to be; young people tell adults about the antics of their friends, about what happened at school. We spin narratives to impart information: How do you make a haggis? Well, you go to the market and you talk to the mutton man. You ask him for the stomach of a sheep.... How did you get that black eye? Well, I was walking home from school, just minding my own business, when.... We tell stories to impart the accepted mores of our cultures to our young. The Old Man Coyote stories of Native American cultures, the cautionary tales of Judeo-Christianity heritage ("The Boy Who Cried 'Wolf!' "), the fables of the slave Aesop are both entertaining and instructive. Every human culture on earth has its fund of stories.

Stories come from many sources but all have their roots in the texture of human experience. A faded photograph has a story, as does a piece of jewelry, a favorite place, an event remembered, and a self that needs to be shared. Stories are the hooks upon which we shape experience and give meaning to the world. A childhood without stories is a library filled with thousands of books with blank pages.

Inside each child is a storyteller just dying to get out. In this book we help the teacher, librarian, or parent unleash the storyteller in each child. The book begins by describing the storytelling process. Each step is accompanied by activities that give students opportunities to practice the skills in creative and fun ways.

Next the reader will explore the many sources of folk literature, including fables and parables, folktales, fairy tales, nursery rhymes, legends, myths, pourquoi tales, children's literature, and urban legends. Activities are suggested that help the teller go beyond the traditional tales to create original works using the forms of folk literature.

The teacher, parent, or librarian will learn how to help children turn factual stories into good telling stories by editing and by finding detail that brings the story to life. Some of the best sources for factual stories are the storytellers themselves. The activities included will help the children get in touch with the stories of their lives and the lives of their families.

Readers theatre gives children another opportunity to work with oral language and story creation. We describe how to create a readers theatre and provide examples of scripts and outlines for script development.

Other chapters include ideas and activities for story creation through pictures, storytelling totes, plateoramas, puppets, and flannel boards and crafts. Often shy storytellers blossom when they can use props such as these.

Even the best storytellers can improve their performances. Thus, the final chapter includes a description of common performance problems with recommended activities for remediation.

Most chapters contain a bibliography of resource materials. The materials may serve as story sources or as a basis for further study. Additional general resources are included at the back of the book.

This book will not only help teachers, parents, and librarians unleash the storyteller in each child, but it will also help children to:

- Improve use of oral language

- Improve listening skills

- Stimulate creative imagination

- Improve visualization skills
- Enhance public speaking ability
- Improve sequential memory
- Enhance writing ability
- Appreciate rich sources of folk literature

In all of these benefits we have not mentioned the one that is the most important. Joyous as it is to watch children enthralled by a good storyteller, more joyous still is it to see children's pride and pleasure as they create and perform their own stories. To see them bow with delight to the applause of their peers, to see them fascinated with the lives of older family members, to hear them laugh at a classmate's fractured fairy tale, to see them sharing of their special selves—here is the greatest of all joys. May this book provide you with the tools to unleash the storyteller in your children so that this joy may be yours.

Acknowledgments

We wish to thank Patty Miller for her time and patience in typing numerous drafts, Jackie DiGennaro for her stories included in chapters 2, 3, and 4, Wayne Gundmundson for providing his photographs for our book, Richard Wells for illustrating the storytelling totes, and our editor, David Loertscher, for his advice and guidance as the manuscript was being written.

1 The Storytelling Process

Many children in our schools today have never heard a storyteller. Junior and senior high school students, in particular, may even be uncomfortable the first few times they hear a storyteller unless they come from a tradition of storytelling. To overcome reluctance, teachers should have students listen to a variety of storytellers, preferably in person. If that is not possible, a teacher may show videotapes of storytellers or share audiotapes with students. After exposure to storytellers, children will want to tell stories, too.

GETTING COMFORTABLE

Although the presentation of a complete story is the goal, we will begin on a much more basic level with the children to build their confidence, skill, and enjoyment in storytelling. In the first part of this chapter, we describe the steps in the storytelling process. Each step is accompanied by a series of activities that will give storytellers an opportunity to practice storytelling skills in a creative and fun way. We begin with three activities that will help children get comfortable in front of an audience. The other steps, with accompanying activities, include visualization, characterization, use of body, voice, dialogue, and pacing.

In this chapter, we also discuss other important aspects of the storytelling process, such as selecting the right story, deciding how much detail to include, mapping stories as a memory aid, learning and presenting stories, warming up for storytelling, and creating an environment for success.

► ACTIVITIES

UP FRONT

Have each child walk to the front of the room, pause, establish eye contact with others, and say, "Hi, my name is _____. And my story is _____." Ask the other students to clap. The speaker bows, pauses, says "thank you," and goes to his or her seat.

FAVORITE OBJECT

Have the children bring a favorite object or a picture of that object. Children will

- name the object;
- explain where or how they got the object;
- say why it is their favorite object; and
- (later as they develop as storytellers) create a story about their object.

JOKES AND RIDDLES

Have children prepare jokes or riddles to tell the class. Ask them to project their voices so that they can be heard throughout the class. Have them visualize that their voice is an umbrella that must cover everyone. The children should stand in front of the group and practice going not too fast and not too slow.

Riddles such as those found in *Biggest Riddle Book in the World* by Rosenbloom (1979) are appropriate for the beginner:

"What is green and dangerous?
A thundering herd of pickles."

"How do you keep a rhinoceros from charging?
Take away his credit cards."

"What is yellow, smooth, and very dangerous?
Shark-infested custard."

Once the children are comfortable standing and talking in front of the room, they can begin to learn the art and craft of storytelling.

VISUALIZATION

Unless the storyteller can visualize the pictures of the story and convey those pictures to the listeners, the storytelling experience becomes a mere recitation of words. If the student is able to create a moving picture in the mind, with each scene materializing as the story progresses, memorizing becomes superfluous. The teller is describing what the teller sees. Gesture and conveyed feeling become completely natural as the teller "lives" the story with the audience. Through voice and action the storyteller conveys the characters, setting, action, feelings, and mood of the story and creates in the listener's mind a mental image, a moving picture of the story.

This step is particularly important for today's television generation. Children desperately need to regain the ability to create images in their mind and describe them to others rather than be passive receptors of television images. The mind's ability to create powerful concrete images is demonstrated by this conversation overheard between two sixth graders:

"John, did you see that neat movie last night?"

"Ya, but I'd read the book and they got the characters all wrong. They didn't look like or talk like that at all."

"They didn't?"

"No, and that's not all, the location should have been different, too. The forest came up much closer to the house, the house should have been brown, not white, and they even changed the ending. There ought to be a law against that."

Visualization brings the story alive. Each telling is fresh and new. The teller can help convey images to the members of the audience by stimulating them through one or more of their senses. These activities will help the students get in touch with their sensory world.

► ACTIVITIES

SENSORY WORDS

Teacher lists the following senses on the board:

	Sight	Hearing	Smell	Taste	Touch
examples:	glowing	shriek	burning	bitter	sharp
	red	blasting	rotten	salty	plush

The students then list all the words they can think of that are part of that sense. Go around the room and have each student select a word and say it in a sentence. Other students listen and let their senses react to the sentence.

OBSERVE, OBSERVE

Divide the class into four groups and assign a sense to each group: sight, hearing, smell, and touch. Have the members of each group observe carefully for fifteen minutes and then describe the room using only their assigned sense.

REACT GAME

Teacher reads a phrase like the ones listed below. The students visualize themselves in that situation and react with facial expressions and movement (and dialogue if appropriate). Students need practice in visualization just as they need practice in math or spelling. These activities are a start.

- A train is moving at sixty miles per hour toward your car, which is stalled on the track—
  React _____
        (name of student)

- Your mother has just walked into the kitchen as you are taking forbidden cookies from the cookie jar—
  React _____
        (name of student)

- You are home with your baby sister, who is upstairs. A fire starts in the kitchen—
  React _____
        (name of student)

- You open a box at Christmastime and in it is a gift you've been wanting for a long time—
  React _____
        (name of student)

- A stranger appears at your door looking very upset. She is carrying your dog, who isn't moving—
  React _____
        (name of student)

- You open your lunch sack and out crawls a green snake—
  React _____
        (name of student)

- A friend dares you to walk through a graveyard. You look over your left shoulder and see something rising up out of the ground—
  React _____
        (name of student)

- You leave school at the end of the day and see the class bully riding away on your bike—
  React _____
        (name of student)

- You have just looked inside your history book for the answer to a question on a test. You look up and your teacher is standing over you—
  React _____
        (name of student)

- Your least favorite teacher absentmindedly walks into a door—
  React _____
  (name of student)

- You are at home and have been trying to solve a math problem for an hour—
  React _____
  (name of student)

Different students could be asked to do the same exercise. The class could discuss how the student reactions were similar or different. Students should notice how each student used body, voice, and action to convey feelings.

Teachers and students should feel free to develop their own *React* statements.

MY FAVORITE PLACE

Students will visualize their favorite places and describe them to partners using as many sensory words as possible. The partners will then tell the original tellers what they saw as the tellers described their favorite places. Then partners switch, with the others describing and the first tellers listening. The teacher will ask if the tellers and the listeners "saw" the same things. How could the descriptions have been better or more vivid?

CHARACTERIZATION

Children will find characterization the most challenging, but ultimately the most satisfying, element of storytelling. The storyteller must create enough distinction among characters to make them clear in the audience's mind. The traits of characters are made apparent through the face, voice, and body movement of the teller. The students should ask the following questions to fully understand each character.

Traits. What kind of person or character is he or she? For example, in "The Three Little Pigs" we know that the first two pigs were lazy and foolish and that the third pig was industrious and wise. What do characters say or do, or what do others say about them, that gives clues to their personality?

Motivation. What motivates each character? For example, King Midas is motivated by his love for gold, by his greed.

Relation to other characters. What is the relation of each character to every other one? What are the family relationships? For example, Cinderella is shunned and enslaved by her stepsisters and her stepmother. Her stepmother favors her two birth daughters.

Purpose. Finally, what is the role or purpose of each character in the story. For example, in the story "Who's in Rabbit's House" the frog is the observer and eventually hops out from behind a tree to solve the problem.

►ACTIVITY

UNDERSTANDING CHARACTER

The teacher should read or tell a well-known story such as "Little Red Riding Hood." The class as a whole should answer the questions posed above. The children should then select a story of their own and answer the questions either in writing or with a partner about each character in the story.

Children need to form a mental picture of the characters in their stories. Even if the author has not fully described the character, it is still important for the teller to be able to visualize each character.

Physical appearance. Describe each character's sex, age, height, weight, clothes, unusual traits, etc.

Voice and speech style. What does each character sound like? Is the wolf in "Little Red Riding Hood" sly and seductive with a sophisticated honeyed voice, or gruff and scary and abrupt? What is the tempo, pitch, and cadence of his speech? Is it small, frightened, and fast like that of the littlest goat in "Three Billy Goats Gruff," or booming, slow, and deep like that of the giant in "Jack and the Beanstalk"?

Contrasts. Have children note the major difference in the characters in the story. The contrasts become useful as the teller tries to distinguish the characters in the telling.

► ACTIVITIES

WHAT DO THEY LOOK LIKE?

After the teacher reads or tells a story, the class should describe the physical characteristics, voice, speech style, and personal qualities of the characters in the story. After students have successfully completed this as a group, have them answer the same questions using a different story. They may either share them with a partner or answer on paper.

WHAT HAPPENED NOW?

After students have selected a story and listed the qualities of the characters, have them select one character and make up a new story in which the character encounters new problems or adventures.

Students should also carefully observe real people in their environment. This will add to the richness of their repertoire of character development and presentation. A character observation sheet follows. Teachers may wish to duplicate the form for each student.

► ACTIVITY

CHARACTERIZATION OBSERVATION SHEET

Observe the following people, either on television or in the community, and fill in the observation sheet.

Character	Unusual or Interesting Phrases in Speech	Sound of Voice	How Walked or Moved	How Dressed
Old Lady				
Old Man				
Small Child				
Athlete				
Young Woman				
Person in Authority, such as Police Officer or Judge				

Many fables, folktales, and fairy tales have as characters animals with human traits, including speech. Children enjoy creating animal characters using their bodies and voices. The following exercise allows for creative development. Teacher may wish to duplicate the form.

►ACTIVITY

ANIMALS ARE SORT OF HUMAN, TOO

Ask children, "If you could be any animal, what animal would you be?" Have them answer the following questions about their animal.

Name of animal _____

What kind of voice would your animal have? _____

How would your animal move? _____

What are the characteristics of your animal? _____

What animal is your animal afraid of? _____

What animals would your animal like to play with? _____

What would your animal's home look like? _____

Write and then tell a story about your animal. Use some of the ideas you gained from answering the questions. Be sure to show how your animal moves.

In addition to knowing and individualizing the characters in the story, children also enjoy becoming one character. The following form could be used for this exercise.

►ACTIVITY

INTERESTING CHARACTER IN HISTORY

Have students list characters in history that they'd like to learn more about. As they read about the character, ask them to answer the following questions:

What do you think your character looked like? _____

What were some of your character's famous deeds? _____

During what period of time did your character live? _____

What was the world like then? _____

What kind of voice would your character have? _____

What would your character talk about? _____

How would your character walk? _____

What things would make your character happy or sad? _____

Invite all of the "characters" to school one afternoon. Each child will assume the personality and interests of his or her character. Children will "talk" about themselves without giving the name of their character. At the end of the day students will guess the identity of each of the characters. This is also very successful with nursery rhyme characters or fairy tale characters.

► ACTIVITY

PERSON ON THE STREET

One of the students is a television announcer who interviews passersby. The questions the announcer asks should be related to a topic the students have studied in class. The teacher writes different characters on 3"x5" cards (for example, a policewoman, a lost child, an old man who is hard of hearing, a woman who considers herself an expert on the subject, a man who is late for work, a jokester). The students draw a card and assume the identity of that person when interviewed.

USE OF BODY

Each storyteller will develop a personal style. Some effective storytellers sit quietly with their hands folded to tell the story. Others move about the space becoming each character. Neither is right or wrong. Gestures and actions need not be planned if the teller has visualized the story. Hands and body will flow naturally. Making a videotape can help students assess their effectiveness. It is better to move too little than to detract from the story with too much movement. The following exercises help students become aware of movement.

► ACTIVITIES

GUESS THE ACTION

Write activities on slips of paper and place them in a box. Have each child draw one slip of paper and act out the activity on that slip for the class. Have the other children guess the activity. Here are some examples:

- Shoveling the snow off the sidewalk
- Eating a banana
- Catching a fish
- Sweeping the floor
- Dribbling a basketball
- Going through a revolving door
- Pouring and drinking milk
- Brushing teeth
- Putting on tennis shoes
- Swimming
- Riding a bicycle
- Painting a picture
- Playing with a hula hoop
- Playing a record
- Playing tennis
- Jumping rope
- Playing hopscotch
- Playing jacks

GUESS THE OBJECT

Write the names of objects on slips of paper and place them in a box. Each child draws a slip and becomes the object. The other children guess the object. Some examples are:

- Popcorn popping
- Washing machine
- Flower growing through the ground
- Tree in a wind storm
- News program on television
- Basketball
- Stapler
- Sewing machine
- Snowblower
- Lawn mower
- Street sweeper
- Can of bug spray
- Wrecking machine
- Chain saw
- Ice cream machine

GUESS THE CREATURE

Write the names of creatures on slips of paper and place them in a box. Have students draw slips and act out the creatures they draw while the other students guess. Examples are:

- Butterfly
- Flea
- Shark
- Kangaroo
- Spider
- Snake
- Buzzard
- Dragon
- Frog

GUESS THE MACHINE

Place in a box slips of paper bearing the names of machines that require two or more students to act them out. Have the students in pairs draw a slip of paper and work together to become a:

- Flashlight (a case containing two batteries, which, when they come into contact with each other, cause a light to go on)
- Power lawn mower (a machine consisting of an engine mounted on top of wheels, a cutting edge powered by the engine, and, on the back, a grass catcher)
- Gum ball machine (consisting of a holder, a crank, gum balls, and a little door that provides an exit for the gum balls when they fall)
- Other (to be made up by students)

LET'S PLAY CATCH

Have students pretend that they are playing catch with balls of different sizes and weights. Have them indicate the size and weight as they catch the following:

- Tennis ball
- Beach ball
- Basketball
- Bowling ball
- Ping pong ball
- Football

MOVE WITH FEELING

Set a chair at the front of the room or in the center of a circle. Have students walk to the chair and sit in it, expressing one of the following emotions:

- Disgust
- Deceit
- Energy
- Delight
- Horror
- Shame
- Fear
- Anger
- Despair
- Frustration
- Pride
- Loneliness
- Boredom

VOICE

Students should be encouraged to use their natural voice for the narrative part of the story. They may vary the pitch, tempo, and emphasis of the voice to individualize the different characters in the story and to reflect the mood of the story. In the following exercises students practice the use of the voice to express emotion and meaning.

► ACTIVITIES

HOW YOU SAY IT

Dorothy Grant Hennings, in *Smiles, Nods and Pauses*, presents an excellent exercise for students to use to practice emotion and meaning. The exercise has two parts. The first part is titled "It's How You Say It That Is Important," and the second is "Say It with Feeling."

Divide the children into pairs. Have the students work first with "It's How You Say It That Is Important." The first student of the pair selects a way of speaking a word or sentence from list 1 and a word to speak from list 2. The second student then says the word expressing that emotion. After the second student has tried the words and emotions, the students switch roles. Then the students try the second exercise, "Say It with Feeling." The student selects a way of speaking a sentence from list 1 and a sentence to speak from list 2. After the first student has completed the exercise, the second student practices with the two lists.

It's How You Say It That Is Important*

I. Ways of speaking a word or sentence:

with sadness	with determination
with regret	with concern
with fear	with lack of concern
with happiness	with enthusiasm
with pride	with vengeance
with disgust	with surprise
with anticipation	with sarcasm

II. Words to speak:

please	often	when	crazy
never	sorry	how	come
good	help	where	no
me	oh	next	yes
you	why	now	stop

*Reprinted with permission from Dorothy Grant Hennings, *Smiles, Nods and Pauses: Activities to Enrich Children's Communications Skills*. New York: Citation Press, 1974.

Say It with Feeling

I. Ways of speaking a sentence:

as if you are expressing a possibility   as if you are in a hurry

as if you are brewing a conspiracy   as if you could care less

as if you are kidding around   as if you are afraid

as if you are threatening   as if you are unhappy

as if you are surprised   as if you are stating a fact

as if you are tired   as if you are fed up

as if you are pleading   as if you are excited

as if you are explaining   as if you are unsure

as if you are disgusted   as if you can hardly wait

II. Sentences to speak:

That program is on tonight.!?

Oh. I'll do that tomorrow.!?

Will you come too.!?

That's a nice dress.!?

I like Suzy.!?

I am going home.!?

Well, let's get started.!?

Why do you bother.!?

I'll see you later.!?

You better not do that.!?

I'll be returning next week.!?

You take care of the money.!?

I'll take care of the supplies.!?

Do you understand what you are doing.!?

Where did you put the candy.!?

Now, everybody, we must work together.!?

INTONATION TELLS ALL

The placement of stress on the words of a sentence can change the meaning of the sentence. For example, let's examine the sentence:

"Are you driving there?"

"Are YOU driving there?" (meaning you, not someone else)

"Are you DRIVING there?" (meaning you are driving, not walking or flying, there)

"Are you driving THERE?" (meaning there, not somewhere else)

The teacher should practice the intonation exercise with several sentences, exploring the different meanings conveyed by the word intonation. The students should practice with a partner, creating their own sentences and meanings.

PARK BENCH

Two students sit in two chairs placed at the front of the room. The other students sit in a semicircle or semicircles facing the chairs. The two chairs represent a park bench where two people meet and carry on a conversation. Students draw cards indicating a mood or personality trait they should assume. Students must stay in character as they converse with their benchmate. After a while a third student taps one of the players on the shoulder, replaces that person, and converses with the person who is still on the bench. The game continues with one person replacing another until all the students have participated. The game ends when the teacher "closes the park." The game can also be played with two strangers sitting on a bus. The following are suggestions for the cards:

- Bored
- Hypochondriacal
- Argumentative
- Friendly
- Worried
- Shy
- Nervous
- Inquisitive
- Happy
- Studious

- Energetic
- Rude
- Depressed
- Angry
- Distrustful
- Impatient
- Uncomfortable
- Upset
- Snooty
- Sensual

- Helpful
- Nurturing
- Interested
- Afraid
- Arrogant
- Busy
- Sad
- Holy
- Disdainful
- Excited

DIALOGUE

Mixing narration with dialogue helps the storyteller create distinctions in character. Since most authors do mix narrative and dialogue, the storyteller simply needs to edit out phrases like "he said" and "she said." Through slight change of voice, the audience will know who is speaking. In creating stories, students may wish to develop dialogue to add interest to the narrative.

►ACTIVITY

ADDING DIALOGUE

The stories that follow have the dialogue removed. To add interest to the stories, have students develop dialogue to go with each of them. Then have the students practice the dialogue in groups. The listeners should give the tellers feedback on the following:

- Can the listener distinguish between characters?
- Does the dialogue help to carry the story line along?
- Does the dialogue add interest to the story?

Little Red Riding Hood

Once there was a little girl named Little Red Riding Hood. One day her dear mother said: (*Add dialogue.*)

And off Little Red went, skipping down the path through the dark woods that led to grandmother's house. She came upon flowers so beautiful that she stopped to gaze more closely at them. She thought: (*Add dialogue.*)

She followed the carpet of flowers into the dark woods picking only the most beautiful for her dear old grandmother. As she reached to pick a particularly beautiful flower she saw a horrible sight. There beside the flower was an enormous black hairy foot. As her gaze slowly lifted she saw that the foot was attached to an evil-looking wolf. His eyes glistened, and his smile revealed rows of knifelike teeth. The wolf said: (*Add dialogue.*)

Little Red said: (*Add dialogue.*)

Little Red continued down the path to grandmother's house. The wolf took a shortcut and got to grandmother's first. The wolf knocked at the door and said: (*Add dialogue.*)

Granny opened the door, and before she could hide, the wolf pushed the door open and gobbled her up in one big gulp. "Now for Little Red Riding Hood," thought the wolf. "I'll have to be clever."
The wolf dressed in Granny's soft blue flannel nightgown and put on her frilly blue nightcap. He crawled into Granny's bed and pulled the covers up under his black nose. Just then Little Red knocked at the door. She said: (*Add dialogue.*)

The wolf, in a sweet Grannylike voice, replied: (*Add dialogue.*)

Little Red entered the bedroom and stared at her grandmother. Granny didn't look at all well. Little Red said: (*Add dialogue between Little Red and the wolf about eyes and ears and teeth.*)

As the wolf leaped out of bed to grab Little Red, he tripped on the nightgown. Little Red screamed for help as she bolted out of the room just out of the wolf's long reach. A woodcutter passing by the house heard Little Red's screams. He broke down the door with his axe and killed the wolf. Little Red found her grandmother's sewing scissors and cut open the wolf's stomach. Out came Granny almost as good as new. Little Red said: (*Add dialogue.*)

And they all lived happily ever after.

Three Little Pigs

Once upon a time there were three little pigs. One day their mother said: (*Add dialogue.*)

Off they went, each to build his own house and seek his own fortune. The first little pig was rather lazy and not very smart. He came upon a man carrying a load of straw. The pig asked: (*Add dialogue.*)

The man said: (*Add dialogue.*)

Before sunset the first little pig had built his house of straw.
The second little pig was also lazy but he was a little smarter than the first pig. He met a man carrying a load of sticks. The second little pig asked: (*Add dialogue.*)

The man answered: (*Add dialogue.*)

The second little pig toiled into the night, and by midnight he had his house of sticks.
Now the third little pig was both smart and hard working. He certainly wouldn't live in a house of straw or sticks. At last he came upon a man carrying a load of bricks. The third little pig said: (*Add dialogue.*)

The man said: (*Add dialogue.*)

The third little pig worked all day and into the night. Just as dawn was peeking over the horizon, the third little pig finished his sturdy house of bricks.

An evil wolf in the nearby forest sniffed the air. "I smell piggies," he thought, wiping the saliva off his lips. Walking in the direction of the strongest scent, he came across the house of the first little pig. He knocked at the door and said: (*Add dialogue.*)

The first little pig answered: (*Add dialogue.*)

The wolf replied: (*Add dialogue.*)

The wolf huffed and puffed and blew the house in. The little pig barely escaped with his life. He ran to the house of his second brother. The wolf knocked at the door and said: (*Add dialogue.*)

The pigs said: (*Add dialogue.*)

The wolf replied: (*Add dialogue.*)

The wolf huffed and puffed and blew the house in. The two little pigs stumbled out of the collapsing house and ran to the house of their brother. The wolf was right behind them. When he reached the house he knocked on the door and said: (*Add dialogue.*)

The little pigs answered: (*Add dialogue.*)

The wolf replied: (*Add dialogue.*)

He huffed and he puffed and he puffed and he huffed and he puffed some more, but he couldn't blow down that house of bricks. The wolf thought: (*Add dialogue.*)

The little pigs heard the wolf crawling on the roof top so they said: (*Add dialogue.*)

The wolf thought he was very clever as he slipped down the chimney. The chimney was hotter than he expected. In a second he found himself in a pot of boiling water. That was the end of the wolf. The first two little pigs soon built their own houses of bricks, and they all lived happily ever after.

PACING

Most beginning tellers talk too fast. Students may wish to tape- or video-record themselves to assess their speed. The teacher will have to stress the need for appropriate pacing. The speed of the telling should flow with the cadence of the story. Thus, as the story reaches its climax, the teller may wish to speed up. Pauses are as important to tellers as words. A pause before a phrase sets up the tension and expectation for what follows. A pause after a significant phrase emphasizes the importance of what was just said and allows the listener to reflect upon it. A pause is also effective to indicate the passage of time or a change of direction in the story.

► ACTIVITY

SETTING PAUSES

The teacher should put a story on an overhead projector. As the class reviews it they should mark with slashes where the pauses should be in telling. Students should then work with one of their stories to set the pauses and try the story with a partner to assess the effectiveness of the pauses.

STORYTELLING WARM-UPS

Before students begin their individual work, the teacher may wish to use some "warm-up" activities with the entire group.

►ACTIVITIES

GROUP STORY CREATION I: THE MAGIC STORYTELLING STICK

Create a magic storytelling stick. It can be a baton, a decorated dowel, or a decorated cardboard tube. Have the class select two main characters, three sensory words, and three emotional feelings from the lists below. Or have them make up their own main characters, sensory words, and emotional feelings. The object of the game is to create a group story that eventually incorporates all of the characters, sensory words, and feelings that were selected. Either the teacher or a student holds the magic storytelling stick and begins the story with two or three sentences. The storytelling stick is then passed to another student who adds two or three sentences to the story. The magic stick is passed around the classroom until either a student or the teacher ends the story. New words can be selected and the game continues.

Main Characters (select one or two of the following or make up your own):

- Abandoned Train
- Hobo
- Porcelain Vase
- Lost Kangaroo
- Reading Book
- Seven-Year-Old Girl
- Old Apple Tree
- Runaway Truck
- Timid Ghost
- Mean Dog
- Pixie
- Talking Rock
- Space Ship
- Skate Board
- Parrot
- Blind Old Man
- Water Slide
- Principal
- Lost Doll
- Lost Airplane
- Bathtub

Sensory Words (select three of the following or make up your own):

- Glaring
- Soft
- Musty
- Messy
- Rusty
- Broken
- Salty
- Sour
- Smooth
- Bright
- Bumpy
- Hairy
- Sweet
- Stinging
- Hot
- Freezing
- Steaming
- Rough
- Flaky
- Uneven
- Dim
- Decaying
- Jumbled
- Creaking
- Grinding
- Itching
- Hungry

Emotional Feelings (select three of the following or make up your own):

- Angry
- Confused
- Excited
- Loving
- Ambitious
- Surprised
- Happy
- Anxious
- Patient
- Sympathetic
- Hurt
- Troubled
- Nervous
- Concerned
- Adventurous
- Afraid
- Irritated
- Terrified
- Bossy
- Affectionate

The lists could also be used for individual telling. In addition, the magic storytelling stick can be used for a group telling a familiar tale such as "The Three Little Pigs."

GROUP STORY CREATION II: TELL THE STORY (UNWIND THE BALL)

The teacher should have cards of three different colors. On one color card the teacher would write plots, situations, or problems. On the second color card the teacher would write the names of characters. On the third set, the teacher would list settings. Thus, the three stacks of cards would cover the following:

1. plot, situation, problem
2. character or characters
3. settings

The students work in small groups. A student draws one card from each stack and shares the cards with the others in the group. Then the student begins to tell the story. He or she can use the magic storytelling stick to pass the story on to the next person or can "unwind the ball." In "unwind the ball," the teacher puts randomly placed knots in a ball of yarn or twine. When a knot appears, the student storyteller passes the ball and the story to another teller.

GROUP STORY CREATION III: STORY IN A SACK

The teacher places three objects in a sack. The objects are taken out of the sack and an individual student or group of students creates a story about the objects.

FIRST SENTENCE

The teacher will want to develop a folder full of first sentences. The sentences can serve as stimuli for either group or individual telling or writing. The sentences can be used with the magic storytelling stick as in the previous exercise. Teachers should encourage students to add to the first-sentence folder. Here is a beginning for your file:

- My baby sister is a real pain. I always wished she'd disappear until one day she...

- I couldn't wait 'til Tuesday. It was the day of the great turtle race...

- One day a little purple man with orange ears and pink hair appeared in my bedroom and said I could have any wish I wanted...

- I never liked Halloween when I was little 'cause I thought all those things were real. My friend and I were out trick or treating last Halloween. Dad said to be home by 8:00 and we were only a little late when we found out the horrible truth in a horrible way—some of the things *were* real...

- Every playground has a bully but ours was the worst. At least he used to be the worst until the day my friends and I decided...

- Everybody should have a pet mouse. I carry Harold in my pocket everywhere I go. Of course my family, teacher, and principal don't know about Harold. That is, they didn't know about Harold until....

LAST SENTENCES

In this exercise students are given the last sentence, up to which they must build the story. This exercise is a bit more difficult than the previous one. Here are some suggestions for last sentences:

- After all that had happened, I didn't care if I ever left my yard again.

- Maybe worms with chocolate syrup aren't so bad after all.

- I still don't believe in ghosts. Or at least I don't think I do—do I?

- And that is how I came to have the name Sara Margaret Elliot Rossetta Jones.

- After that they'll never ask me to play in another piano recital.

- After all we'd been through together, I couldn't take that mongrel dog to the dog pound. I'd convince Dad somehow.

- And there was the bottom of my swimming suit stuck on the top of the water slide.

- After that we never saw the extraterrestrials again.

- It was the happiest day of my life.

SELECTING THE RIGHT STORY

Storytelling folklore says, "Storytellers don't pick stories, stories pick storytellers." A story that works well for one storyteller may not work well for another. Finding the right story may be largely a matter of trial and error.

The most important question for a teller to ask is, "Do I like this story?" There is a wide variety of tales to chose from: folktales, fairy tales, myths, legends, fables, fantasy, and modern literature—both fiction and nonfiction. The teacher may want to preselect thirty or forty stories for the children to chose from. The teacher must remember that a good story for telling has a different emphasis and construction than a story written for reading. What is a good tellable tale? The story should have:

1. One central plot uncluttered with secondary plots. Each incident must follow logically one from the other, creating clear and vivid pictures in the mind of the listener. Stories with flashbacks or long descriptive passages that interfere with the flow of the story should be avoided.

2. A variety of sensory and visual images. The story should create a "movie in the mind" as it is shared with the audience. The language should be beautiful, descriptive, and colorful.

3. A limited number of characters.

4. Colorful characters who are interesting and believable or, in the case of the traditional fairy tale, who clearly represent qualities such as greed, beauty, and goodness.

5. Emotional appeal, courage, love, laughter, suspense, excitement, sentiment, and plenty of action.

6. A strong introduction that motivates the audience to listen. It also should set the time and place, create the tension in the story, and establish the mood. If the story is good but the introduction is weak, the teacher should help the students construct an opening that grabs attention, sets the theme and mood, and leads swiftly into action.

7. A satisfying conclusion.

HOW MUCH DETAIL?

Effective storytelling requires a balance between including enough detail to make the story live in the listener's mind and including too much. Extraneous material, no matter how interesting, can detract from the primary theme of the story. In everyday life as people share stories with each other, boring tellers usually include too much or inappropriate detail. Therefore, teachers must work with students to help them find the balance.

Students must be able not only to cut out extraneous detail, but also to add interesting detail to stories to make them live.

► ACTIVITIES

A HUNT FOR INAPPROPRIATE DETAIL

The teacher should put a folktale or fairy tale on the overhead projector. As a group, the students should hunt for and delete detail that adds little or nothing to the story. As they look for the core of the story and the action line, they may wish to:

• Eliminate unnecessary description

• Tighten sequence of the action

• Simplify explanatory passages

• Clarify or eliminate confusing passages

ADDING DETAIL – JUST THE FACTS

Several stories with the detail removed are included on the following pages. Put one story on an overhead and work as a class to develop interesting and appropriate detail. Then have the students try the exercise with a different story, either alone or with a partner.

Just the Facts—Rumpelstiltskin

- Miller very poor—one day brags to King that daughter can spin straw into gold.

- King demands she be brought to castle and put to the test.

- Girl put in a room with spinning wheel and spindle—if straw not spun to gold in morning she will die.

- Little man appears—does work—she pays with necklace.

- Next morning King astonished and greedy—puts her in larger room with same command.

- Little man appears, does work, and is paid with her ring.

- King takes her to a larger room to spin straw to gold or die. If she is successful, he will marry her.

- Little man appears—miller's daughter promises her first-born child.

- In a year King and Queen have child—little man comes to collect.

- Queen upset so little man gives her three days to guess his name.

- Messengers go out to bring back all the names.

- Each day guesses get more bizarre.

- On the final day a messenger says a little man is dancing around a fire chanting,
  "Today do I bake, tomorrow I brew. How fortunate that
  no one knew that Rumpelstiltskin is my name.
  The Queen's child will be my claim."

- Queen guesses and Rumpelstiltskin is so mad he stomps his foot and disappears deep into the earth.

Just the Facts—Elves and Shoemaker

- Shoemaker so poor only had enough money left to make one pair of shoes. He cut out the shoes intending to make them in the morning.

- In the morning he found the shoes done without a stitch out of place.

- A man bought the shoes—paid more than ordinary price. The shoemaker could buy leather for two pairs of shoes with the money.

- He cut out the shoes in the evening and in the morning they were done.

- He sold them for enough money to be able to buy leather for four pairs.

- The next morning four pairs were finished. So it went until he became a well-to-do man.

- One night near Christmas the man and wife sat up to see who was lending a helping hand.

- At midnight two little naked men sat down and stitched, and sewed, and hammered, and finished, and ran away.

- The wife said that they must show their gratitude and she made little shirts, coats, waistcoats, stockings, and a pair of shoes for each.

- She left them out that night—the shoemaker and wife hid to see how they'd react.

- The elves were surprised and delighted. They sang, "Now we're boys so fine and neat. Why cobble more for other's feet?"—and they hopped and danced!!!

- They came no more but the shoemaker had good luck in all of his undertakings.

Just the Facts — Bremen Town Musicians

- Dog had grown old and was going to be put to death because he was no longer useful.

- Ran away to Bremen to be a town musician.

- Collected cat, donkey, and rooster who were also old and about to be done away with.

- Animals grew tired and hungry and saw a light shining in the distance.

- Looked in window and saw that there was a robbers' den that had delicious food and drink and money.

- Animals developed a plan to scare robbers out. Outside the window the
      dog got on the donkey's back
      cat got on the dog's back
      rooster got on the cat's back

- On signal they performed their music:
      donkey — brayed
      hound — barked
      cat — meowed
      cock — crowed

- The robbers, thinking it was a demon, ran out.

- Animals ate heartedly, then found a sleeping place:
      donkey — outside
      hound — beside the door
      cat — on hearth
      cock — in rafters

- The robbers came back and crept into the house; thinking the cat's eyes were coal, robber held a match close and burned the cat.
      — cat flew at face, spat and scratched
      — tripped over dog — dog bit his leg
      — donkey kicked him with hind legs
      — cock awoke, cried out from perch — — — — Cock-a-doodle-doooo!

- Robber ran to his chief and told of monsters in the house:
      — a witch who scratches with long fingers
      — by door a man with knife who stabs
      — outside black monster hits with club
      — on the roof is a judge who cries, "The Judge Will Git YOU!!"

- The robbers never went back to the house. The animals lived there the rest of their lives.

Just the Facts—Queen Bee

- Three princes set out to seek fortune—two were mean to their youngest brother they called Blockhead—thought they were so much smarter.

- Two elder brothers wanted to:
    - destroy an ant hill—Blockhead stopped them
    - kill some ducks swimming about—Blockhead stopped them
    - set fire to a tree and suffocate the honey bees that lived within—Blockhead stopped them

- Came to castle where all people had been turned to stone except a strange little gray man who had bewitched all of the people.

- If princes could complete the three tasks, they could free the castle of the spell; if not, they too would be turned to stone.

- *First task*: In the woods, princesses' pearls, a thousand in number, had to be found before sunrise or the seeker would be turned to stone.

- Two older brothers failed and were turned into stone.

- Blockhead was failing too when the Ant King, whose life he had saved, sent 5,000 ants and all pearls were found.

- *Second task*: Get princesses' key out of the bottom of the lake.

- Ducks he'd saved—dove until they found the key.

- *Third task*: Blockhead had to discover which princess was youngest and most charming though they looked alike and were stone.

- Before they were turned to stone, the eldest had eaten sugar, the second had eaten syrup, and the third had a spoonful of honey.

- Queen of Bees who had been saved licked the lips of each princess and told Blockhead which had eaten the honey. Blockhead identified the youngest one correctly.

- Evil spell broken—all were set free.

- Blockhead married the youngest and sweetest princess and became King after her father's death.

- Two brothers married other sisters.

Just the Facts—Frog Prince

- Princess favorite toy was golden ball.

- She dropped it in well—heartbroken.

- Ugly Frog agreed to get it if princess would let the frog:
    1. be her playmate
    2. sit at her table
    3. eat off plate
    4. sleep on her pillow

- Frog got ball—princess ran home.

- While eating dinner knock at door—princess trembles.

- Frog tells king of princess's promise—king makes princess keep promise.

- She's disgusted but agrees and does 1, 2, 3; can't stand thought of frog on pillow but finally agrees.

- When he touches pillow frog turns into a prince.

- He'd been bewitched by an evil queen. Spell could only be broken by a fair maiden permitting 1, 2, 3, 4.

- Fell in love—lived happily ever after.

STORY MAPPING—A USEFUL MEMORY AND ORGANIZATIONAL TOOL

The brain, that highly efficient and effective microcomputer, stores experience and knowledge in complex categories and networks within its cells. This knowledge of how the brain stores and retrieves information can be capitalized on by the storyteller to create and easily remember stories. By drawing a one-page map or schema of the story structure, the teller will have a graphic picture of the story as a whole, which can be stored in the conscious memory for easy recall. Brain researchers tell us that the use of images can raise memory performance to near perfect and multiply creative thinking effectiveness by as much as ten times (Buzan, 1988). The map and the way the brain stores and remembers information are then much the same (like using compatible programs for a computer). The visual nature of the map, the need for good visualization for good storytelling, and the brain's existing networks complement and connect one with the other.

The story maps can be created in many ways. The teller may develop a tree-like map to organize the story structure, the main ideas, and the pertinent supporting details of the story (see fig. 1.1); or the teller may draw a map like a treasure hunt, linking the scenes of the story together (see fig. 1.2). "Little Red Riding Hood" is given as an example in figures 1.1 and 1.2.

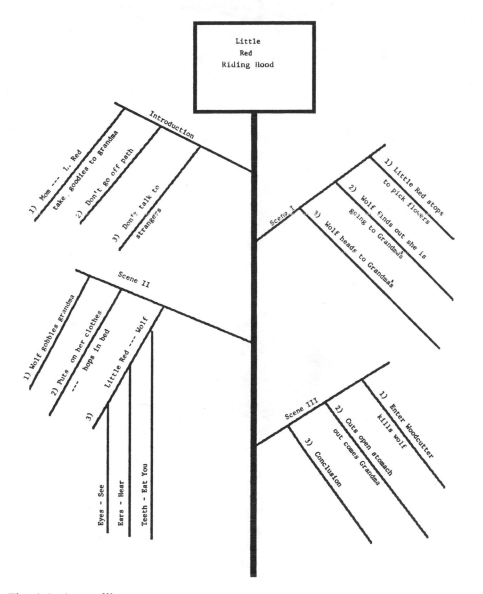

Fig. 1.1. A tree-like map.

Little Red Riding Hood

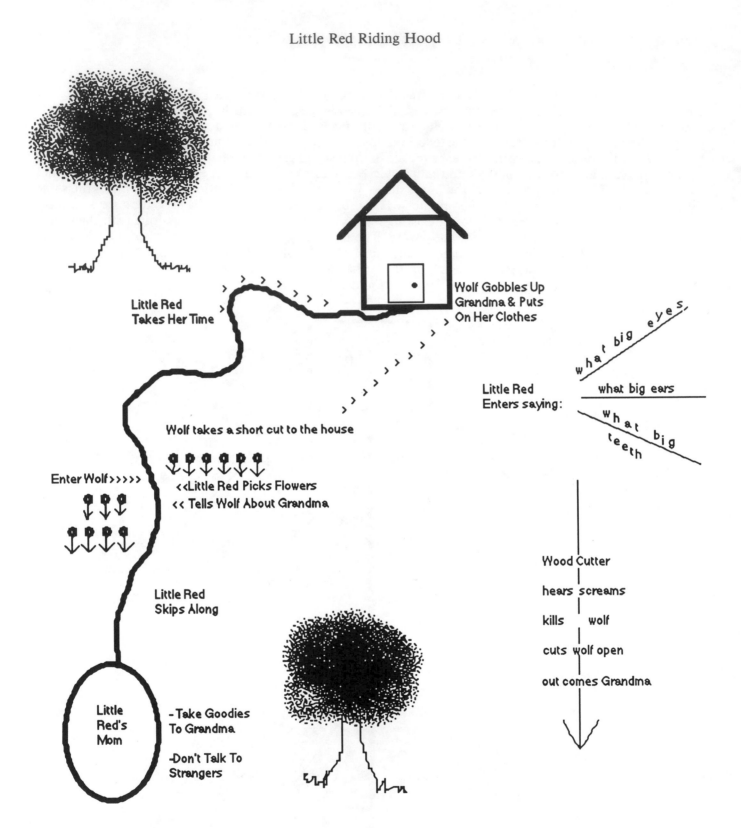

Fig. 1.2. A treasure-hunt map.

Another configuration might be the filmstrip approach showing individual scenes (fig. 1.3). This approach might be particularly suitable for young children.

Fig. 1.3. A filmstrip.

An example of another map, this one for the book *Jumanji* by Chris Van Allsburg, is shown in figure 1.4.

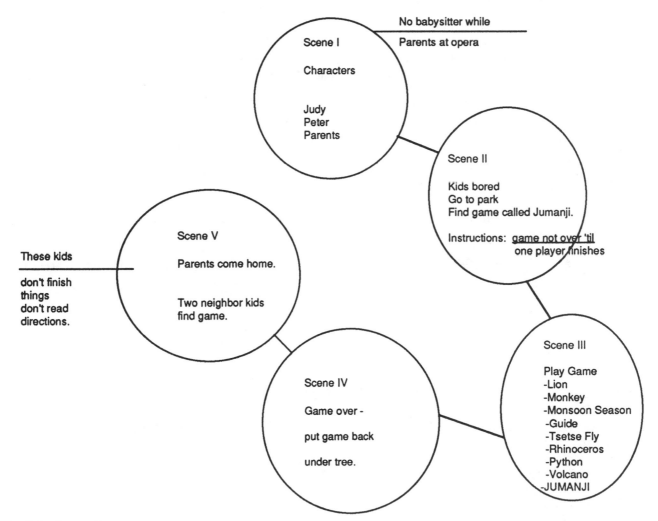

Fig. 1.4. *Jumanji* map.

Whatever type of story mapping the teacher chooses to use, the students will find it a valuable process for story memory and story analysis.

LEARNING AND PRESENTING STORIES

Stories should *not* be memorized, rather they should be learned. The teller takes the story into his or her heart and gives it back as a gift to the audience. The story is shared through the teller's own words except for repetitious phrases, rhymes and poems, and beginning and ending sentences. If the story is memorized, it may lose its spontaneity and freshness in retelling. Interruptions can throw the teller off course. Fortunately, learning and presenting stories is much easier than one might imagine. Teachers should help students through the following straightforward steps:

1. Find or write a simple story that you truly enjoy.

2. Read the story several times, both silently and orally.

3. Put the story away and visualize the story. Make a movie in your mind imagining the character, setting, and action.

4. Think through the sequence of events. Make a story map or outline of the story.

5. Think through the characterization of each person in the story. How will you distinguish one from another? Do you need to add dialogue? Is there extraneous detail that doesn't add to the story?

6. How will you begin and end the story? Are there any of the author's phrases that you want to be sure to use?

7. Read the story again. Then, using the outline or story map, tell the story out loud without an audience.

8. Put the map or outline down and say it again out loud. If you get stuck, refer back to the outline or the map.

9. Practice one more time, alone. You may wish to tape yourself and review the tape, listening for gaps in the story.

10. Tell the story to a small group in the classroom.

11. You are a storyteller.

CREATING AN ENVIRONMENT FOR SUCCESS

The teacher plays a key role in ensuring student success. Here are a few tips on creating a positive environment:

1. Start students with baby steps so they are successful at each step of the process. Begin with some of the simplest and least threatening exercises in this book. Even in later stages, students may be more comfortable hiding behind a prop, a costume, or a puppet. Suggestions are included throughout this book.

2. Storytelling should be fun. It should not be graded or tested, nor should the stories become reading lessons.

3. Establish a ritual that takes the children to the magic of story time: light a candle, get on a magic carpet, wear a storyteller's hat, play some special music, close the shades, use a special corner—anything to break the routine. Have students get ready to enjoy each other's stories.

4. Keep interruptions to a minimum. If you can, turn off the intercom or ask that you not be interrupted except for an emergency. Put a Do Not Disturb sign on the door. Students may lose their train of thought if interrupted.

5. Be positive!

CONCLUSION

This first chapter has examined the storytelling process. The subsequent chapters will show ways for children to create their own stories as well as to use the many rich sources of literature.

BIBLIOGRAPHY

Creative Dramatics/Theatre

Hennings, Dorothy Grant. *Smiles, Nods and Pauses: Activities to Enrich Children's Communications Skills*. New York: Citation, 1974.

Mapping

Buzan, Tony. *Super-Creativity: An Interactive Guidebook*. New York: St. Martin's, 1988.

Heimlich, Joan E., and Susan D. Pittelman. *Semantic Mapping: Classroom Application*. Newark, Del.: IRA, 1986.

Riddles

Rosenbloom, Joseph. *Biggest Riddle Book in the World*. New York: Sterling, 1979.

Using Literature as a Basis for Storytelling

Much of the literature we enjoy today, such as folktales, fairy tales, myths, fables, and legends, came from the oral tradition. Many of these tales were first shared orally among the people of the times, and only later were they collected and recorded by folklorists and anthropologists. Because the tales were first told orally, many of them are compact—already edited from years of telling—and thus easy for students to retell.

In this chapter, the reader examines various types of folk literature: fables, folktales, fairy tales, nursery rhymes, legends, myths, pourquoi tales, children's literature, and urban legends. The chapter includes many activities to help the teller move beyond the oral retelling of a story into original story creation using the various forms of folktales. Nine original stories serve as examples for creating new stories using the traditional forms of folk literature. A bibliography citing works for each of the various types of folk literature concludes the chapter.

FABLES AND PARABLES

The terms "fable" and "parable" are virtually interchangeable. Both are short tales that communicate a truth or teach a lesson about life. Fables generally convey practical wisdom, often using animals as the main characters. A parable, which means "the word," usually explores a more serious theme, often teaching a moral or a religious principle. Parables tend to be more realistic than the fanciful fable. The best-known fables are those of Aesop. By placing the moral at the end, Aesop tells the readers what they are supposed to learn from the tale. However, such explanation is not always desirable or required.

► ACTIVITIES

RETELL A FABLE

The teacher should read a variety of fables to the students. A list of resources is included at the end of the chapter. Students can then read fables on their own and select one to retell in their own words to a small group. The other students can guess the moral of the story.

MODERN FABLES

Students will enjoy writing and telling their own modern fables. The teacher reads several modern fables to the students, such as the three that follow. The teacher and the students discuss how Pelton developed a story using a familiar moral. Students learn how they too might structure original fables for telling. Students may wish to retell one of Pelton's fables in their own words.

Who Says Pigs Can't Climb Trees?

Mary Helen Pelton

Once there was a large pink pig named Harold who liked nothing better than to bask in the sun, sniff the flowers, and watch the butterflies play in the wind. His friend George pig said, "Let's find a way out of this pen so we can stroll in the woods."

"It's impossible to get out of here except through the gate, and besides (zzzzzzz)," said Harold. And before he finished he was sound asleep. Soon Marge, the farmer, opened the gate so Harold and George could get a bit of exercise. Harold was not very fond of exercise so he walked four feet from the pen and lay face down to rest.

"Come on, Harold," said George. "Let's figure out how we can get across the ravine. The apples look so wonderful on the trees on the other side. Let's cross the ravine, climb the tree, and feast on apples."

"It's impossible to get across the ravine. It's so wide and deep, and besides, in case you haven't noticed, pigs can't climb trees. You're a little slow, George," said Harold.

"What do you mean I'm slow?" said George. "I'll race you to the ravine and we'll see who's slow."

"Race! Race! Surely you jest," scoffed Harold. "Pigs can't race. They can scamper perhaps, but race never. Greyhounds, horses, and small children race. Pigs waddle, stroll, and as I said before, we occasionally scamper. Very occasionally!"

Farmer Marge finished cleaning the pen. "Harold, George, time to get back in the pen. Harold! Harold! Harold, wake up and get back in your pen." Harold waddled in and plopped down in the soft new hay and stretched out to catch the rest of the afternoon sun.

Late that evening George and Harold were awakened by a scraping, scratching sound coming from the far end of the pen. A hole appeared on the inside of the fence, then a furry paw, then a pointy nose with long, sharp teeth glistening in the moonlight. A head appeared with red and yellow eyes above the smacking lips of an evil wolf.

"Come little piggies, piggies, piggies. Come to nice Wolfie," cooed the wolf as he pulled himself out of the newly dug hole reaching for the pigs.

"We've got to get out of here," yelled Harold as he scampered over the fence just out of the reach of the wolf. He pulled George after him. The two pigs raced toward the ravine. "Hurry," yelled Harold, "throw that log over the ravine. We need a bridge to get to the other side."

Once across the ravine, the pigs pushed the log bridge into the gully hoping that would stop the wolf. But the wolf was long and lean and with one powerful leap he sailed across the ravine without missing a step. The pigs could feel the wolf's hot breath on their haunches as he grew closer and closer.

"Can wolves climb trees?" puffed George.

"I don't think so," answered Harold. "Quick! into the apple tree."

And before you know it both of them had climbed up the tree. The wolf snarled and howled in frustration. The pigs' tails dangled just out of his reach. Farmer Marge heard the commotion and raced out with a shotgun. One shot and Wolfie was gone.

"Hmm," said Marge retracing the pigs' escape. "I didn't know that pigs could climb out of the pen, outrun a wolf, bridge the ravine, and climb trees. Well, I'll be darned. You learn something new every day, don't you?"

Moral: Necessity is the mother of invention, or, You never know what you can do 'til you have to.

Two Brothers

Mary Helen Pelton

Once there were two brothers. One was very vain and one was very kind. Albert, The Vain, got up every afternoon at one p.m. He needed his beauty sleep. After arising he combed his long brown hair and servants brought him garment after garment. He fussed and fussed trying on this one then that one, trying to get just the right color combination and the right look to suit his mood. Four hours later he strolled vainly out to court. He threw back his head and strutted down the long amber carpet looking this way and that way, but greeting no one. Instead, he admired his resplendent reflection in the mirrors of the great hall.

His brother, Samuel The Good, on the other hand jumped out of bed at 5:30 a.m. There was so much to do. He raced to the village to help a goodly, but very old, man start his fire to warm his house in the wee hours of the morning. He saw an old grandmother trudging along hauling water for her grandchildren. Samuel grabbed the buckets from her frail arms and carried them to her house before she could catch her breath. A young mother wailed because one of her twins had toddled out of the house while she was changing the other one. She feared that the child had fallen into the river. Samuel hurried to the river and found the little one wading into the deep water calling "Nice froggies, nice froggies." Samuel gathered him up in his arms, kissed him, and handed him back to his mother.

A beggar, homeless and alone, passed by Samuel. Samuel gladly took off his coat, gave him all the breakfast that he had in his pack and his lunch as well before he walked on to see who else might need his help. He told stories to a blind man confined to the house to help him pass the time. He helped a young mother hang her wash after a horse had pulled it down. He said, "Let me help," to a young boy whose cows had escaped during the night. To a young monk who toiled in the garden, he said, "Let me help." And thus he toiled, dirty, hungry, wet, and happy, until after midday.

As noonday passed he walked back to the castle and entered his brother's room and said, "Dear brother you should be arising now. I must tell you the news of the day."

As Samuel walked down the splendid hall with Albert, Albert glared at his brother, "Sam, you are a wreck. Look at you. You are dirty, you are wet, you are not at all like a prince."

Samuel looked at his own reflection in the mirror. "You're right Albert, but you look good enough for both of us."

Just then a green light flashed in the hall and before them stood a radiant woman truly as elegant and handsome as Albert. She said, "I am the most beautiful of the fairy queens and I will choose the handsomest prince in the land to be my husband."

"That would be him," said Samuel.

"That would be me," said Albert, tossing back his hair, again looking at his reflection.

Suddenly outside a woman screamed as a wagon lost its wheel and tipped over on her husband. Samuel rushed out to help.

"Yes," said the fairy queen, "you are clearly most handsome." She tapped Albert on the head with her magic wand, immediately turning him into a large green toad wearing the clothes of a prince. Then the fairy queen changed into her true toad form.

"Where is the other prince?" she croaked. "I need another prince as a servant."

"Yes, get him," croaked Albert. "He doesn't look too great but you'd like him better. He is always doing good deeds."

"I detest good deeds," said the fairy queen, who was as ugly on the inside as she was on the outside. She invited all of the people of the kingdom to share in their wedding feast of flies and mosquitoes. Tears appeared in the eyes of Toad Albert when he saw his hideous image in the mirror.

"I hate flies," croaked Albert.

When the time came for the prince to take over the kingdom, the people showered praises upon Samuel, who ruled the realm with dignity, grace, fairness, and love. As for Albert, he dwells in the swamp with the fairy queen and is doomed for the rest of his life to look at his own hideous reflection in the water of the swamp.

Moral: It is better to be good than to look good.

Home for the Bear Family

Mary Helen Pelton

Once there was a family of bears who was very dissatisfied with their home. The bears lived in a dark, cool cave on the far side of a green grassy hill.

"It's too drab," said Sister Bear.

"It's too cold," said Mama Bear.

"It's too dark," said Papa Bear.

Mama Bear looked out the door of the cave at an eagle's nest on a far-off hill. "Look at the bird's nest; it's open and soft," said Mama Bear.

"Not at all like a cave," said Sister Bear.

"Let's move," said Papa Bear. And they did. You should have seen all three bears trying to squeeze into an eagle's nest. And just as they finally got themselves arranged, it started to rain.

"Too wet," said Sister Bear.

"Too drafty," said Mama Bear.

"Too crowded," said Papa Bear.

"Well, how about a beaver's house? It would be cozy and warm and safe from intruders. Not at all like a cave. Let's move," said Sister Bear. And they did, but Sister Bear had a hard time holding her breath long enough to get inside, and Papa Bear got stuck in the entrance.

"Too damp," said Mama Bear.

"Too muddy," said Sister Bear.

"Too small," said Papa Bear.

"How about a dog house?" said Mama Bear. "People would feed us every day, and we'd have lots of company from all the neighborhood kids."

"Let's move," said Sister Bear. So they did. All day long the neighborhood children raced and hollered as they tore through the yard. Every evening the bears were brought a huge bowl of steaming dog food.

"Too noisy," said Sister Bear.

"Too drafty," said Mama Bear.

"Too much dog food," said Papa Bear.

The bears move from the dog house to a squirrel's hole in a tree; from the squirrel's hole they tried a rabbit's den. And from there they tried a large bird house. As Papa Bear perched, looking not quite in and not quite out of the bird house, he spotted a cave on the side of the green, grassy hill. "Let's move there," he said. And they did.

"It's wonderfully quiet," said Sister Bear.

"It's so gently dark," said Mama Bear.

"It's roomy," said Papa Bear, "and you know what else, it sure feels like home." They nodded and stretched out contentedly, and as far as I know they're still there.

Moral: Nothing looks as good as home after a long absence, or, The grass is always greener on the other side of the fence.

CREATE A FABLE FROM A MORAL

The teacher writes morals on cards or gives the students a list of morals. Teachers may duplicate the list on p. 32 for this purpose. The students write or record their original tales, practice them and tell them to a small group.

YOUR ORIGINAL FABLE

The students write or record either an original fable or a parable that teaches a lesson or shares wisdom. The students practice telling the story and then share it with the group. Although fables and parables need not have an explicit moral, listeners might guess the lesson.

Morals

A fool and his money are soon parted.

The early bird gets the worm.

A rolling stone gathers no moss.

A stitch in time saves nine.

An apple a day keeps the doctor away.

You'll never know a man until you've walked a mile in his moccasins.

Better to be good than to look good.

Nothing ventured, nothing gained.

One good turn deserves another.

What does around comes around.

You'll never see the wonder of the sky if you stare only at your feet.

Like father like son.

Things are not always as they seem.

You made your bed so you have to sleep in it.

The grass is always greener on the other side of the fence.

A bird in hand is worth two in the bush.

It is easy to despise what you know you cannot possess.

Clothes may disguise a fool until he opens his mouth.

A hero must be brave in deed as well as in word.

Birds of a feather flock together.

Evil wishes have evil consequences.

Where force fails, patience will often succeed.

It is well to know one's guest before offering him hospitality.

Half a meal in freedom is better than a full meal in bondage.

Deeds are far more convincing than boasts.

Look before you leap.

There is always someone worse off than ourselves.

There is no believing a liar, even when he speaks the truth.

United we stand; divided we fall.

In union there is strength.

Remember not to trust those who praise you falsely.

It is better to be content with half than to lose all.

It is far better to bend than to break.

Those who tell falsehoods sooner or later find themselves in deep water.

FOLKTALES

Folktales are stories that mirror human behavior. They speak of the human condition—its joys, sorrows, trials, loves, struggles, fears, and celebrations. Folktales usually reflect the culture and the people of the land from which they come.

► ACTIVITIES

TELL A FOLKTALE

The teacher reads or tells a number of folktales to the class. (A list of resources is included in the bibliography at the end of the chapter.) The teacher then preselects thirty or forty "tellable tales" from which the students will select a tale to learn and tell to the class.

WHICH VERSION DO YOU LIKE BEST?

Students read several versions of the same tale. Have them discuss which version they like best and why? Ask them to compare cultural names, places, objects, and customs unique to each story. Parallel stories can be found by using indexes in *World Folktales: A Treasury of Over Sixty of the World's Best-Loved Folktales* by Atelia Clarkson and Gilbert B. Cross, New York: Scribner, 1980; *The Types of the Folktale: A Classification and Bibliography* (2d ed., rev. 1961) by Antti Aarne and Stith Thompson, Helsinki: Folk Lore Fellows Communications #184, 1961; and *Type and Motif-Index of the Folktales of England and North America* by Ernest Baughman, The Hague: Mouton, 1966. Have students tell their favorite version.

NEW FROM OLD

After reading several folktales, ask students to examine the structure of the tale. Have them, using the form of the tale, put the story in a different culture, either their own culture or one that they are studying in social studies. Jackie DiGennaro, a teacher in Sitka, Alaska, patterned her "Tlingit Canoe Story" after the folktale "The Little Red Hen." First she mapped out the characters, plot, and dialogue in the familiar folktale.

Characters

Red Hen	Cat
Goose	Pig

Plot

Hen finds a grain of wheat. Hen decides that it would make a fine stalk of wheat if she plants it. Hen asks for help in planting the grain but is turned down by Goose, Cat, and Pig. She decides to do it herself. Hen plants the grain. In time, she needs help reaping the wheat. Hen asks for help from Goose, Cat, and Pig but is turned down. She reaps the wheat herself. Next, Hen needs help carrying the wheat to the mill to be turned into flour. She asks for help from Goose, Cat, and Pig, but she is refused again and carries the wheat to the mill alone. Hen needs help turning the wheat into bread but is again turned down by her companions. Finally, Hen asks for help in eating the bread. This time, Goose, Cat, and Pig are happy to comply, but Hen refuses to let them share in the fruits of her labor, and she enjoys the fresh-baked loaf by herself.

Dialogue

Hen, at each stage of her task, asks, "Who will help me?"

Every character replies in turn, "I won't," said the _____.

Finally, when Hen asks, "Who will help me eat the bread?" all the characters answer, "I will," said the _____ , "I will," said the _____ , etc.

Hen replies, "You didn't help me plant the grain. You didn't help me reap the grain. You didn't help me bake the bread. Now I will eat the bread by myself."

After mapping out the story of "The Little Red Hen," DiGennaro replaced the characters with cultural figures from a southeastern Alaska Indian tribe called the Tlingit. Hen became a Tlingit elder, who finds not a piece of grain but a cedar tree in the forest, which may become a fine canoe. He returns to ask for help from his sister and nephews, who refuse to help him fell the tree, float it back to the village, and carve the tree into a canoe. Thus, when a volcano erupts, and the canoe is needed to paddle to safety, the elder travels alone across the water, leaving his indolent family behind. This is the story Jackie DiGennaro created.

Tlingit Canoe Story

Jackie DiGennaro

Long ago, before the white man first came to the land in their giant canoes with great sails, a Tlingit elder came upon a tall, stately cedar in the forest. "This tree will make a fine canoe!" he thought to himself, "but I will need much help to fell the mighty cedar." So he went back to his clan house, where his sister and his two nephews all sat, warming themselves by the fire."

"Who will help me cut the tree?" asked the elder, as he stooped to enter the house.

"I won't," answered his sister. "I would rather fill this basket with plump salmonberries from the forest." And she left with her basket of tightly woven spruce root, to hunt for the yellow-gold salmonberries in the woods.

"I won't," replied his older nephew. "I would rather spear the salmon where the river runs swift and shallow." And the boy left, carrying his spear with its sharp wooden point, baked hard and deadly in the coals.

"I won't," said his younger nephew. "I would rather hunt for shells on the beach, where the waves spit them out on the sands." And so, too, the younger boy left, with his pouch of deerskin, for gathering the indigo mussels and twinkling abalone shells.

So the old man returned to the forest and felled the cedar by himself, but first he thanked the spirit of the tree for giving its life to his family, and asked the spirit's forgiveness on them for their laziness.

Wearily, he then returned to his clan house and curled up on his blanket, shutting out the loud snores of his family.

The next morning he asked his family, "Who will help me float the log back to our village?"

"I won't," said his sister, who was weaving a blanket from the coarse, stiff hair of the mountain goat.

"I won't," said his older nephew, who was skinning the salmon he had caught in the stream.

"I won't," said his younger nephew, who was carefully poking holes through shells to string them on a necklace.

So the elder returned once more to the forest. After much pushing and pulling, he eased the log into the water, where he floated it across the bay to his village.

"Who will help me carve the canoe?" he asked of his family when he returned.

"I won't," said his sister, who was practicing a dance, bobbing and weaving, with her beautiful new blanket draped across her shoulders.

"I won't," said his older nephew, who was smoking the bright red strips of salmon he had filleted the day before.

"I won't," said his younger nephew, who was busy admiring the handsome reflection of his new necklace, in the water of the stream.

So the old man carved and carved until he had a fine canoe. He said nothing, but one anguished tear left his eye and trickled down his proud cheek until it splashed on the gunwale, where it left a dark stain.

That night, the unhappy spirit of the tree whirled and danced about the lodge. It coursed through the dwelling, causing the woman to cry out in her sleep and clutch her blanket tightly around her. It rattled the necklace of the younger nephew, who had hung it carefully on a peg beside his bed. It blew on the cinders in the smokehouse, sending ashes and soot to cling to the fish hanging there to cure.

Only the old man slept peacefully, a sad little smile twitching the corners of his mouth.

The spirit danced across the bay, where it awoke the greater spirit of the volcano we now call Edgecumbe. The sister spirit grumbled and sighed, and spewed fire and smoke from her depths in sympathetic anger.

The Tlingit elder and his family awoke in fear as the red-hot cinders rained down upon their lodge.

"Who will paddle with me to safety?" asked the old man as he shoved the canoe to the water's edge.

"I will!" shouted his sister, as she tossed her blanket into the canoe.

"I will!" answered his older nephew, who threw what salmon he could salvage into the canoe.

"I will!" said his younger nephew, as he laid his beautiful shell necklace carefully on the seat.

"No," replied the old man sadly. "You didn't help me fell the tree. You didn't help me float the tree. You didn't help me carve the tree. Now I must paddle to safety alone."

And so, without a backward glance, the elder took up his paddle and traveled to safety across the water, while the cries of his family blended with the whine and moan of the spirits, until he could no longer tell one from the other, and he was alone.

After writing the tale, DiGennaro asked Peter Corey, museum curator for the Sheldon Jackson Museum in Sitka, Alaska, to review the tale for cultural authenticity. She then revised the tale based on his recommendations.

Students following a similar pattern would not only enhance their writing and telling skills, but would also gain cultural insights and sensitivities in a most meaningful way.

Sometimes students have a mental block when it comes to story writing. Giving them a starting point, by working with a familiar folktale or fable, is one way to overcome "writer's block."

USE THE STRUCTURE

Have students examine the structure of several folktales. Using the structure as a pattern, they should write or record, then tell, their own tales. Several common structures are listed below:

Structure I: Main character sets out on a quest and helps a less fortunate person who will later help him or her. Three tasks are put before the main character. With the help of a less fortunate one, the task is accomplished. The evil is destroyed or the prize is won.

Structure II: Least likely character takes central action (stupidest, youngest, poorest, worst-treated). Character is somehow shown most worthy and finds good fortune: wins the trial, wins the prize, earns the kingdom.

Structure III: The main character through magic is given three wishes. Through the character's own foolhardiness or greed, the opportunity is lost and the character ends up worse off than before.

Structure IV: A person dies with unfinished business on earth and therefore can't rest even in death. The ghost haunts the living until the brave soul figures out the ghost's problem. Once the business is taken care of the ghost goes to its eternal rest.

Structure V: The little man sets himself against the rich and powerful Establishment and wins the quest through cunning and trickery.

Structure VI: Before the peasant girl can marry the rich lord she must first impress him with her extraordinary wit and intelligence.

Structure VII: Main character is given an impossible task. With the help of a supernatural helper the task is accomplished and the reward is won.

POINT OF VIEW

The student can tell a familiar tale from another character's point of view:

Story	Point of View
"Little Red Riding Hood"	Wolf
"Goldilocks and the Three Bears"	Littlest Bear
"Three Billy Goats Gruff"	Troll
"Hansel and Gretel"	Stepmother or Wicked Witch
"Rapunzel"	Witch
"Three Little Pigs"	Wolf

A NEW PERSPECTIVE

Students can use their favorite folktale character and create a new adventure with a different problem or resolution.

WHAT IF?

Using a familiar folktale the students can examine the tale from a new perspective to create a new tale based on What If...? Would this new factor change the story? How? For example: What if the wolf in "Little Red Riding Hood" had been a vegetarian? What if Jack in "Jack and the Beanstalk" had not chopped down the beanstalk in time? What if the wolf in "Three Little Pigs" had had asthma? What if the wicked witch in "Hansel and Gretel" has been very kind as well as beautiful and loving? What if the prince in "Cinderella" had turned out to be a real bum? What if Rapunzel had been a boy? Have the students make up their own "what ifs" and share them with the group.

FAIRY TALES

Most of the fairy tales in the English-speaking world were inherited from stories about the Celtic fairies, pixies, elves, imps, sprites, gnomes, brownies, and leprechauns. Magic and the supernatural are part of the lively plots.

► ACTIVITIES

FIND A FAIRY TALE

The teacher reads several fairy tales to the class. (A list of resources is included in the bibliography at the end of the chapter.) The students read stories on their own and select one for retelling to a small group. The teacher may wish to preselect tales that are easy to learn.

FRACTURED FAIRY TALE

Students can take a favorite tale, rewrite the story in a modern context, and share their fractured fairy tale with a small group.

A DIFFERENT PLACE

Students can study the structure of a fairy tale and place the tale in a different country, perhaps a country they are studying in social studies. The setting, customs, and problems should reflect those of the new country.

NURSERY RHYMES

Even nursery rhymes can be a source for storytelling. Have you wondered what the "real" story is behind a rhyme. Maybe the children have, too.

►ACTIVITY

THE STORY BEHIND THE RHYME

Students read several nursery rhymes and create a story about what is behind one of the rhymes. Or they might create a story about what happens where the rhyme leaves off. Examples of these two approaches follow.

Little Miss Muffet
Mary Helen Pelton

Little Miss Muffet sat on a tuffet eating her curds and whey.
Along came a spider and sat down beside her
And frightened Miss Muffet away.

Once there was a little girl named Angela Muffet who liked to brag that she wasn't afraid of anything. Her brother put a big frog in her bed, and she laughed and chased the poor frog all throughout the house. One night when she was sleeping her brother covered himself with a bed sheet, stood at the end of her bed, and woke her up with moans and chain rattling. This time she chased him throughout the house. He put snakes in her shoes, let a bat go in her bedroom, left scary notes all around the house that a monster was coming to get her, and Angela just laughed and said she wasn't afraid of *anything*. Then one day, Angela was sitting outside under the apple tree in a beanbag chair eating cottage cheese when a tiny spider, no bigger than a grain of rice, floated down on his almost invisible string. He landed like a whisper right in the middle of Angela's cottage cheese. Angela tried to scream but no sound came out. After several minutes of paralyzed fear, Angela threw the bowl and ran into the house. Her brother watched and thought, "Well ol' Angela is afraid of something after all." He climbed down from his tree house with a jar and immediately began hunting for spiders.

Jack and Jill
Mary Helen Pelton

Jack and Jill went up a hill to fetch a pail of water.
Jack fell down and broke his crown
And Jill came tumbling after.

Jack and Jill lived in a little cottage at the base of a steep hill. Each day the children climbed the tall hill to draw water from the well for their dear mother. "Always follow the long path, dear children, for the short cut is very dangerous. Your father fell there three years ago and lost his life. I couldn't bear to lose you too."

For years Jack and Jill did just that. But one day they were in a hurry and they took the shortcut. They jumped from unstable rock to unstable rock. Suddenly a rock shifted throwing Jack thirty yards below. The crack of his head hitting the rock awoke the fairy people who lived in the dark places of Middle Earth. As Jill attempted to help him, she too tumbled and fell. Both children would have died had it not been for the curiosity of the fairy people. The fairy people poked their heads out of the rocks to find what had made the loud noise. Tears filled their tiny eyes when they saw the children lying still at the base of the hill. Fairies are very fond of children and particularly of Jack and Jill, so they formed a fairy circle around the wounded children and chanted...

Children we watch day and night
Are wounded and hurt and still
Around them weave our magic light
So their lives they might fulfill.

And as the children's eyelids began to flutter and life came back to them, the fairy people scurried back to their dark hiding places.

LEGENDS

Legends are stories about people, places, or events believed to be based on historical fact. The character or event becomes embroidered with detail and exaggeration until the character or the event is larger than life. American literature has evolved a specific type of legend called a tall tale, which seems to express an attitude typical of the United States. The characters are larger and stronger than life. The tales are usually a balance between truth and untruth in favor of untruth. The tales contain local color with circumstantial detail. The tales tend to be bragging or boasting and are rich with colorful language. Legendary characters include such people as:

- Johnny Appleseed, based on a person named John Chapman, who really did tramp through the Ohio Valley

- Paul Bunyan, not a real person but the invention of an advertising man in the 1920s to promote the Red River Lumber Company

- Pecos Bill, cowboy, and Joe Magarac, steelworker, invented in the early 1900s

- Casey Jones, a real person who did indeed courageously sacrifice his own life to save the lives of his passengers

- John Henry, a black railroad worker remembered for his formidable physical powers

- Davy Crockett, a frontiersman, who really did live in the early 1800s

Other real people who have passed into legend include outlaws (Belle Starr, Billy the Kid, Jesse James, Sam Bass) and giants who were larger than life (whaler Old Stormalong; riverboaters Annie Christmas and Mike Fink; fisherman Barney Beal; farmer Febold Feboldson; and frontierspeople Calamity Jane and Daniel Boone).

► ACTIVITIES

FIND A LEGEND

Have the students read several legends or tall tales. (Several good sources are included in the bibliography at the end of the chapter.) Have them retell a story in their own words.

CREATE A LEGEND

Have the students create a new tall tale or legend placing the hero or heroine in a new setting with new adventures, friends, or problems. Have them tell their tale to the group. An example of such a tale follows.

Paul Bunyan and the Blizzard of 1892
Mary Helen Pelton

The temperature had been hovering around ninety-seven degrees below zero for six weeks. Even Paul and the boys couldn't go out in weather like that. The big lumbermen were getting right cranky and mean from being cooped up like a bunch of angleworms in a bait can.

Sam Redeye was particularly cantankerous, "Mighty Luke, you are breathing too loud; a fellow can't hear himself think."

"What do you mean too loud, you ugly frog. If I looked as bad as you, I wouldn't care if I ever breathed again," hollered Mighty. Mighty didn't even have time to blink. A huge pillow hit him square in the face and burst in an explosion of goose down. Mighty hurled a pillow back at Redeye knocking off his hat and his pipe.

Before you knew it all the boys had picked up pillows and were pounding the daylights out of each other. Pillows were exploding like fireworks on the Fourth of July. Goose feathers were flying everywhere. Just then a huge wind came up and picked up the feathers turning them into huge snowflakes. The Great Blizzard of 1892 began.

Within three days those goose down snowflakes covered the state we now call Minnesota with twenty-five feet of snow and with it the temperature rose to a warm two below zero.

As soon as the blizzard stopped, the boys started digging out Babe, the Blue Ox, and the other livestock. If it hadn't been for the Big Thaw they'd be digging still. But then, that's another story.

LIAR'S CONTEST

Have a Liar's Contest where the students assume the identity of one of the characters in a legend or tall tale and try to outlie each other. A bibliography of tall tales is included at the end of the chapter.

LEGENDARY CHARACTERS

Have students brainstorm the names of local or state individuals who have become or are becoming "legendary." Have students create a new story about that person, weaving together fact and fiction. Stories can be shared in small groups.

LEGENDS AND PLACES

Many places (towns, rivers, mountains) have legends associated with them. Have students research the facts behind a place near their home and then create a legend about it. Owatonna, Minnesota, has a lovely legend explaining how the town got its name.

Legend of Owatonna

Mary Helen Pelton

The spirits had been good to the tribe lead by the mighty warrior Chief Wabena; but one winter the snows came with a howling vengeance driving the deer and the other game to safer grounds. Day after day the hunters returned empty-handed. There came a time when the children cried in pain against their hunger. Sickness and death stalked the tepees as one by one the people chanted, "Obewana wana," (I go, I go) and made their final journey to the spirit world.

Chief Wabena's daughter, Owatonna, was much loved by the people, not only for her dark brown eyes and gentle ways, but also for her trilling laughter which made even the most somber among them smile. In the deep of winter, sickness visited the chief's tepee. Owatonna's voice grew quieter until at last only a whisper could be heard from her sickbed.

"We can withstand much sadness but not the sorrow of losing our beloved Owatonna," whispered the people outside her tepee. The chief sent for the medicine man, Chewadala. He mixed brews of birch bark, balsam, and wintergreen and gave them to Princess Owatonna. Though he called upon the spirit healer, Owatonna only grew weaker. The people kept a silent vigil outside her tepee.

At last an old one came forward and took the chief aside, "When I was a girl, my father's father spoke of Minnewaucan (curing water) which gushed from the earth in a bubbling fountain. The ancient ones said that those who would drink from the magic curing waters would be filled with health and long life. It is told that the waters are southward through the valley of the great rivers."

Chief Wabena commanded the people to prepare at once for the journey in search of the waters. Those who were too sick and weak to walk were carried on travois. Southward they trekked across rivers and prairies until they came to a place where the oak, maple, and birch called to them. As they looked across the stream, they saw the wondrous waters gushing from the earth flowing into sparkling pools.

Chief Wabena gently lifted the head of Owatonna so she could drink from the curing waters. "Drink deeply, my daughter. The sparkle will return to your eyes and the flush to your cheeks and strength to your limbs," said the chief.

For many days thereafter Owatonna did as she was bid and life returned to her. Spring brought back life to the earth, too. The hunters found plentiful game. Such was the joy and the contentment of the people that they dwelled there for the rest of their days.

Many years have passed since then. Indian lore tells us that Owatonna's kindly spirit still hovers near the spot to beckon weary travelers to pause in the beautiful valley and drink deeply of the cool, life-giving waters. The people of Owatonna built a statue in honor of the princess at the base of the bubbling waters. Some say that you can still hear her laughter in the gentle murmur of the waters as they find their way to the great river which leads to the sea.

LOCAL HAUNTS

USA Today featured "Local Haunts" in its October 31, 1989, issue. The article, reprinted here, describes ghosts from each state that have passed into legend. After reviewing the article, students should write a tale about their favorite ghosts or write a legend about ghosts from their state.

Local Haunts*
USA Today

Every state has its own ghost story, tales told by local inhabitants about long-ago residents who are said to prefer their old homes to the hereafter. Experts scoff, but here are some legends that live on this Halloween night:

ALA: Banks of Choctawhatchee River, Newton: A hole dug to hang Confederate Army deserter in 1864 is said to be cursed by his ghost. Campers who fill the hole claim they awake to find it "swept out clean."

ALASKA: Gakona Lodge and Trading Post, Gakona: Pipe-smoking ghost, possibly of a construction worker who built some of the buildings, is said to haunt log structures.

ARIZ: Former Army officer's quarters, Nogales: Helpful ghost of a U.S. soldier who served during skirmishes with Geronimo is known for cleaning up messes at U.S. Army Post.

ARK: The Old State House, Little Rock: Frock-coated ghost said to stride through the Old State House, believed to be Representative Anthony, murdered by Speaker Wilson in 1837.

CALIF: The Whaley House, San Diego: Haunted by ghosts of Thomas and Anna Whaley. Anna checks doors and windows. Also heard: heavy footsteps, a woman singing.

COLO: The Former Bradley House, Denver: Late Hubert Work, secretary of Interior under President Harding, supposedly rocks rocking chair, levitates lamps, slams doors.

CONN: The Ledge Light, off New London: "Ernie," lighthouse keeper of 75-year-old lighthouse, is still there. He unties boats, moves coffee cups. Ernie jumped to death from lighthouse when his wife ran away with another man.

DEL: The Governor's House, Dover: Mansion built in 1770 is crowded with apparitions: a wine server, a Revolutionary War colonel, a slave kidnapper, even a girl in red gingham.

D.C.: Decatur House, Washington: Commodore Stephen Decatur, Jr., an 1812 war hero who died in 1820 from dueling wounds, has been seen brooding in a bedroom window.

FLA: Ashley's Restaurant, Rockledge: Young woman in 1920s clothing is said to appear in powder-room window.

GA: Dobbins Air Force Base, Marietta: Legend says a ghost of an Englishman who committed suicide in 1880 resides in a three-story wood and brick office building.

HAWAII: Waters off Waialua, Oahu: Lone fishermen hauling in nets on beaches are attacked by the Mo'o, a woman with lizard-like features and long, reptilian tongue.

IDAHO: An old downtown building, Genesee: Haunted by huge rat, whose mummified body was found under kitchen floor.

ILL: Resurrection Cemetery, Justice: "Mary" has been seen here in a ballgown and dancing shoes since her burial here following a car accident in 1934.

IND: Indiana Dunes State Park, Lake Michigan: For more than 70 years, visitors have reported seeing ghost of "Diana of the Dunes" hurrying over the sands at twilight.

IOWA: Mathias Ham House, Dubuque: Nineteenth century house is known for its icy winds, unexplained voices and electric lights that reportedly turn themselves on and off.

KAN: Kansas State University, Manhattan: Ghost of "Nick," a college football player who died here in the 1950s, supposedly talks on tape machines; footsteps heard in halls.

KY: Liberty Hall, Frankfort: Haunted by helpful "Gray Lady," in gray dress, who does household chores, gazes out windows.

LA: Oaklawn Manor, Franklin: Southern belle spotted strolling here caused a duel between Civil War soldiers.

MAINE: Beckett's Castle, Cape Elizabeth: Stone cottage haunted by Sylvester Beckett, prominent artist, publisher and lawyer, who is said to take paintings off walls and open doors.

MD: The Edgar Allan Poe House, Baltimore: Old, heavy-set woman dressed in period costume haunts the plain, two-story house built in 1830 and once inhabited by famous author.

MASS: John Stone's Inn, Ashland: $10 bills said to materialize in tip jars behind the bar; flying china, taps on shoulders occur at this inn built in 1832 by wealthy land owner Capt. John Stone.

MICH: Gotschall's Inn: Ghost of lighthouse keeper William Pryor, who disappeared in 1901 after apparent suicide, runs basement shower in this lighthouse inn on Lake Superior.

MINN: St. Mary's College, Winona: A dorm named after Bishop Patrick Heffron is said to be plagued by footsteps, tappings, cold spots caused by priest who died in 1943 while being institutionalized for attempting to kill Heffron.

MISS: Deserted mansion, Gulfport: An unseen performer, possibly young daughter of Harriet Gibbons, who committed suicide, plays Chopin on the piano in the music room.

MO: Knob Noster: Ghost of an old hermit haunts the area. He is supposedly seen during every storm descending a hill toward the town with his lantern swinging back and forth.

MONT: Grandstreet Theatre, Helena: Friendly ghost of a pastor's wife moves stage props in a playful way in the theatre.

NEB: Omaha Indian Reservation, Blackbird Hill: Belief persists that the chilling scream of a woman murdered by her jealous husband can be heard each year on Oct. 17.

NEV: Goldfield Hotel, Goldfield: Gold Rush era hotel, once the most magnificent west of the Mississippi, is said to be haunted by spirit of murdered, pregnant woman chained to a bed.

N.H.: 19th century house, Gilsum: The house is haunted by young man who lived there before dying in the Civil War. He's said to sit in kitchen, turn lights on and off.

N.J.: Victorian mansion, Midland Park: Civil War era mansion haunted by a number of ghosts including that of a yellow and white cat who leaves warm spots.

N.M.: The Lodge, Cloudcroft: Haunted by the spirit of a waitress killed in the 1930s by her lumberjack lover. They say she lights up switchboards, turns on faucets and moves furniture.

N.Y.: State Capitol, Albany: The Assembly chamber of Capitol, built in 1868, is long thought haunted by Sam Abbott, a night watchman who died in 1911 fire here.

N.C.: Public Library, Wilmington: Apparition of local historian is said to open file drawers in the historical wing of the library.

N.D.: Liberty Memorial Building, Bismarck: The ghost of Civil War Gen. William Henry Harrison Beadle is seen sitting in a classic car near where his statue once stood.

OHIO: Stetson House, Waynesville: Ghost of Louisa Stetson Larrick, sister of famed 19th-century hat maker John Stetson, has been reported dissolving into walls.

OKLA: Stone Lion Inn, Guthrie: Ghost of F. E. Houghton's 8-year-old daughter, accidentally poisoned by a maid, rearranges toys in locked closet, covers dolls in 200-year-old cradle.

ORE: The White Eagle Cafe, Portland: Ghost who flushes toilets in men's rooms thought to be Sam, son of tavern's early owners. Sam died of natural causes at 30.

PA: Loudon Mansion, Germantown: Haunted by benevolent ghosts of two former residents. "Willy," the ghost of playful 11-year-old, rearranges books and hides expensive china.

R.I.: The Sprague Mansion, Cranston: Security guards at this 18th-century mansion are said to be tormented by a former butler who yanks covers off the beds.

S.C.: The Hermitage, Murrells Inlet: It's haunted by spirit of broken-hearted "Alice" who loved a turpentine salesman against the wishes of her brother. Legends says Alice searches for her lost engagement ring on moonlit nights.

S.D.: The Green Door Brothel, Deadwood: Ghost of young prostitute, murdered by customer in 1920s, walks the halls.

TENN: Carnton Mansion, Franklin: Lone Confederate soldier walks in the house and marches around the yard of this mansion, near where 1,481 Confederate soldiers are buried.

TEXAS: Writer's and Artist's Retreat, Denton: Since 1974, residents report seeing apparition of large dragon. Legend says area is Indian burial ground.

UTAH: Denver & Rio Grande Railroad Depot, Salt Lake City: Woman, who died on train tracks trying to retrieve engagement ring thrown by angry fiance, is seen in ladies room.

VT: Shard Villa, Salisbury: This gothic-style mansion built in 1870s by lawyer Columbus Smith is supposedly plagued by ghosts who unlock doors. Ghosts could be Smith's son and daughter who died young and are buried in nearby crypt.

VA: Scotchtown, Beaverdam: 18th-century home of Patrick Henry is said to be haunted by his first wife, Sarah Henry, who was confined to the cellar because of mental illness.

WASH: Rosario Resort, Eastsound: Ghost of Alice Rheem, who drank too much and was unfaithful to her husband, is heard cavorting in her old room in mansion on isolated island.

W.VA: St. Peter's Church, Harpers Ferry: On misty nights, the dying words of a wounded Civil War soldier, "Thank God I'm saved," can reportedly be heard at the threshold of the church.

WIS: The Grand Opera House, Oshkosh: Ghost of man wearing turn-of-century clothing is seen carrying a playbill for *The Bohemian Girl*, which played there in 1895.

WYO: St. Mark's Episcopal Church, Cheyenne: Legends says ghost of a 19th-century immigrant is still heard and felt in the bell tower of the church. He died during the building of the tower and was bricked into the wall by his friend.

Compiled by Jane McClaran and Edward Findlay.

MYTHS

Traditionally, myths are stories that were created by primitive people to explain natural phenomena or to relate how social, political, or sacred customs developed. Myths, usually set in the remote past, attempt to explain such things as the origin of the world, humankind, and the unseen, powerful forces of nature. They are poetic alternatives to scientific accounts.

The Greek, Roman, and Norse cultures have been major sources of our most familiar myths. These myths, along with stories from the Judaic and Christian religions, are an important part of our religious heritage. Joseph Campbell (1988), in his book *The Power of Myth*, says that we should read myths for several reasons. He believes that myths basically serve four functions:

- Mystical function—realizing the wonder of the universe, the wonder of self, and experiencing awe before this mystery

- Cosmological function—showing the shape of the universe but showing it in such a way that the mystery lives

- Sociological function—supporting and validating a certain social order

- Pedagogical function—teaching humans how to live their lives

In recent times the myths of the Native American, as well as myths from the cultures of the Eskimo, the Kono, the African, and other peoples, have been collected and retold. An excellent example of such a collection is Virginia Hamilton's book *In the Beginning* (1988). The myths in her book tell of the acts of creation—of the universe, of the gods of many cultures, of our world, of a new beginning, and of humankind in a "time before time."

► **ACTIVITIES**

FIND AND RETELL MYTHS

The teacher reads or tells myths from various cultures to the students. (A number of good sources are included in the bibliography at the end of the chapter.) Students then read myths on their own and tell them to a small group. Have students compare the themes of the myths from different cultures.

OLD MYTH—NEW SETTING

Have students select a myth from one culture and rewrite or retell it from a different cultural perspective. They may use either their own culture or one they are studying in social studies.

POURQUOI, OR HOW AND WHY, STORIES

Pourquoi tales, closely related to myths, explain how and why a physical or cultural phenomenon began. Animal pourquoi tales explain how animals came to have various characteristics.

► **ACTIVITIES**

HOW AND WHY OF THE ANIMAL WORLD

The teacher reads several tales about how animals came to have certain characteristics. Students read the stories on their own and retell them. Next they create original tales using the formula:

Why the *(name of animal)* has *(a particular feature)* .

ORIGINAL POURQUOI TALES

The teacher reads or tells other how and why tales to the students. (Several good sources are included in the bibliography at the end of this chapter.) After students have read several tales on their own, they are ready to create and tell their own pourquoi tales.

Have students list the things they wondered about when they were little. They select a topic and write, then tell, an original pourquoi tale that explains that natural phenomenon. Students could also research the real scientific explanation. Some possible questions are:

- What causes the northern lights?
- Why are snowflakes so perfect?
- What makes the leaves change color in the fall?
- How do spiders know how to spin their webs?
- What causes thunder and lightning?
- Why are the people of the earth so many different colors?
- How did peacocks get their color?
- What do dogs dream about?
- What happens to the other sock in the dryer?

- How do birds know when to migrate?
- What happens to words after they're spoken?
- Where does the wind start?
- Why is a flame coolest in the middle?
- Where do colors come from?
- Where did man find fire?

An example of such a tale follows.

What Happens to the Other Sock?
Mary Helen Pelton

My mother says she just doesn't know what happens to the other sock in the washer and dryer. She says she often ends up with one less sock when she takes the socks out than when she put them in. Last year, alone, she ended up with fourteen unmatched socks. I know the answer but I don't think I'd better tell her 'cause she wouldn't believe me.

In a time before people counted time, little people lived beneath the pine tree and wild flowers in the very place where our house now rests. The earth was very warm then so the little people did not wear clothes. Over time the earth got colder and colder so the little people had to dig down and live in the Middle Earth where the temperature stays warm all the time. Even though they were happy there, they longed to see the bright sun and the beautiful sky.

One day, although it was winter on earth, the little people felt a warm breeze blowing in their ceilings. The leader of the little people tunneled up and came face to face with a big black hose that was blowing hot air. Using strong hooks the leader crawled inside the black hose until he was inside a big machine that was filled with warm fluffy socks. When one landed on him it felt like the softest petal of a summer rose. He took the sock back to Middle Earth and found that by cutting off a hole in one end he could pull it over his head and he had a wonderful warm robe. Everyone else wanted a long fuzzy robe, too.

Day after day the leader would go back to the earth and bring back more socks. He was so small he could carry only one sock at a time. Soon all the little people will have robes, then they'll be able to return to the earth and enjoy the sun and beautiful sky.

As for me, I just hope they hurry up and take the railroad socks my Grandma gave me. They'd look better on them than they do on me.

CHILDREN'S LITERATURE

Children's literature, both picture books and longer works, provides many rich opportunities for the storyteller.

► ACTIVITIES

MY FAVORITE PART

Children orally retell a favorite part from a library book. This is an excellent way to teach them to summarize and edit. A time limit, say five minutes, should be placed on the presentations. As always in good teaching, the teacher demonstrates the process before the children try it on their own.

WHO WILL BUY?

Children create a radio or television advertisement for their favorite book. The presentations can be tape-recorded or videotaped for added authenticity.

URBAN LEGENDS OR MIGRATORY TALES

Urban or modern legends are oral accounts of improbable events that never really happened but are often told as true (or attributed to a friend of a friend) and embellished with local detail. Folklorist Jan Harold Brunvand has written four well-documented books with fascinating tales of these supposedly "true" stories (see chapter bibliography). Junior and senior high students will particularly enjoy working with these tales and tracking down the urban legends in their own communities.

►ACTIVITIES

WHAT'S REAL?

After the teacher or students have read several urban legends, students can compile similar stories they have heard told as truth. They can compare and contrast the accounts they have heard and prepare one for retelling to a small group.

WHAT'S IN THE NEWS?

Students can watch the newspaper for urban legends and compile a notebook of them for future retelling. For example, on February 17, 1990, the *Grand Forks (N.D.) Herald* ran a story exposing one of the newest urban legends. Supposedly the news media had uncovered a new cult of toad-licking people in California; however, after much searching, reporters could not locate a primary source. The tale, told by friends of friends, has now entered the annals of urban legends.

CONCLUSION

The creation of new stories and the retelling of old ones based on the world's rich heritage of literature are limited only by teachers' and students' imaginations. In the next chapters readers will explore other stimuli for story writing and telling.

BIBLIOGRAPHY

Fables

Berrill, Margaret. *Chanticleer*. Illustrated by Jane Bottomley. Milwaukee: Raintree, 1986.

Bierhorst, John. *Doctor Coyote: A Native American Aesop's Fables*. Illustrated by Wendy Watson. New York: Macmillan, 1987.

Castle, Caroline. *The Hare and the Tortoise*. Illustrated by Peter Weevers. New York: Dial, 1985.

Hague, Michael, comp. *Aesop's Fables*. New York: Holt, Rinehart and Winston, 1985.

Lionni, Leo. *Frederick's Fables* (A Leo Lionni Treasury of Favorite Stories). New York: Pantheon, 1985.

Lobel, Arnold. *Fables*. New York: Harper, 1980.

Miller, Edna. *Mousekin's Fables*. New York: Prentice Hall, 1982.

Reeves, James. *Fables from Aesop*. Illustrated by Maurice Wilson. New York: Bedrick/Blackie, 1985.

Simon, Seymour. *Animal Fact, Animal Fable*. Illustrated by Diane deGroat. New York: Crown, 1979.

Stevens, Janet. *The Town Mouse and the Country Mouse*. New York: Holiday House, 1987.

Fairy Tales

Andersen, Hans Christian. *The Wild Swans*. Illustrated by Susan Jeffers. New York: Puffin, 1981.

Braekstad, H. L., trans. *Hans Christian Andersen's Fairy Tales*. Illustrated by Hans Tegner. New York: Beekman House, 1978.

Collins, Meghan. *The Willow Maiden*. Illustrated by Laszlo Gal. New York: Dial/Pied Piper, 1988. (Picture book)

Dickinson, Peter. *The Iron Lion*. Illustrated by Pauline Baynes. New York: Bedrick, 1984.

Eisen, Armand. *Goldilocks and the Three Bears*. Illustrated by Lynn Bywaters Ferris. New York: Knopf/Borzoi, 1987. (Picture book)

Galdone, Paul. *Rumpelstiltskin*. New York: Clarion, 1975. (Ages 4-9)

Goodall, John S. *Little Red Riding Hood*. New York: McElderry, 1985. (Wordless)

Grimm, Jacob, and Wilhelm Grimm. *The Elves and the Shoemaker*. Retold by Bernadette Watts. Salt Lake City: North-South Books, 1988. (Picture book)

_____. *The Golden Goose*. Adapted by Anthea Bell. Illustrated by Dorothee Duntze. Salt Lake City: North-South Books, 1988. (Picture book)

_____. *Snow White and Rose Red*. Retold by Bernadette Watts. Salt Lake City: North-South Books, 1988. (Picture book, ages 6-9)

_____. *The Twelve Dancing Princesses: Retold from a Story by the Brothers Grimm*. Illustrated by Susan Jeffers. New York: Dial, 1981.

Haley, Gail E. *Jack and the Bean Tree*. New York: Crown, 1986. (Picture book)

Hodges, Margaret. *Saint George and the Dragon: A Golden Legend*. Illustrated by Trina Schart Hyman. Boston: Little, Brown, 1984. (Ages 6-10)

Hogrogian, Nonny. *The Glass Mountain*. New York: Knopf, 1985.

Hyman, Trina Schart. *The Sleeping Beauty*. Boston: Little, Brown, 1977.

Lesser, Rika. *Hansel and Gretel*. Illustrated by Paul O. Zelinsky. New York: Dodd, Mead, 1984.

MacDonald, George. *The Golden Key*. Illustrated by Maurice Sendak. New York: Farrar, Straus, 1976.

Marshall, James. *Goldilocks and the Three Bears*. New York: Dial, 1988.

_____. *Red Riding Hood*. New York: Dial, 1987.

Mayer, Marianna. *Beauty and the Beast*. Illustrated by Mercer Mayer. New York: Four Winds, 1979.

McKinley, Robin. *Beauty: A Retelling of the Story of Beauty and the Beast*. New York: Harper, 1978.

Owens, Lily, ed. *The Complete Brothers Grimm Fairy Tales*. New York: Avenel, 1981.

Perrault, Charles. *Cinderella*. Illustrated by Marcia Brown. New York: Scribner, 1954.

Philip, Neil. *Drakestail Visits the King: A Magic Lantern Fairy Tale*. Illustrated by Henry Underhill. New York: Holiday House, 1986.

Rogasky, Barbara. *The Water of Life: A Tale from the Brothers Grimm*. Illustrated by Trina Schart Hyman. New York: Holiday House, 1986.

Scieszka, Jon. *The True Story of the Three Little Pigs*. Illustrated by Lane Smith. New York: Viking-Penguin, 1989.

Waddell, Martin. *The Tough Princess*. Illustrated by Patrick Benson. New York: Philomel, 1986.

Wiesner, David, and Kim Kahng. *The Loathsome Dragon*. Illustrated by David Wiesner. New York: Putnam, 1987.

Folktales

Botkin, B. A., ed. *A Treasury of American Folklore*. New York: Bonanza, 1983.

Calvino, Italo. *Italian Folktales*. New York: Harcourt Brace Jovanovich, 1980.

Clarkson, Atelia, and Gilbert B. Cross. *World Folktales*. New York: Scribner, 1980.

Cole, Joanna. *Best-Loved Folk Tales of the World*. Illustrated by Jill Karla Schwarz. New York: Anchor, 1982.

Cooper, Susan. *The Silver Cow (A Welsh Tale)*. Illustrated by Warwick Hutton. New York: Atheneum, 1983.

Crossley-Holland, Kevin, ed. *Folk Tales of the British Isles*. New York: Pantheon, 1985.

Cushing, Frank Hamilton. *Zuni Folk Tales*. Tucson: University of Arizona Press, 1986.

Demi. *The Hallowed Horse (A Folktale of India)*. New York: Dodd, Mead, 1987.

Glassie, Henry, ed. *Irish Folk Tales*. New York: Pantheon, 1985.

Hamilton, Virginia. *American Black Folktales*. Illustrated by Leo Dillon and Diane Dillon. New York: Knopf, 1985.

Lester, Julius. *The Tales of Uncle Remus—The Adventures of Brer Rabbit*. Illustrated by Jerry Pinkney. New York: Dial, 1987.

_____. *More Tales of Uncle Remus—Further Adventures of Brer Rabbit, His Friends, Enemies, and Others*. Illustrated by Jerry Pinkney. New York: Dial, 1988.

Nagishkin, Dmitri. *Folktales of the Amur—Stories from the Russian Far East*. Illustrated by Gennady Pavlishin. New York: Abrams, 1980.

Phelps, Ethel Johnston, ed. *Tatterhood and Other Tales*. Illustrated by Pamela Baldwin Ford. New York: Feminist Press, 1978.

Singer, Isaac Bashevis. *Stories for Children*. New York: Farrar, Straus and Giroux, 1984.

Taylor, Mark. *The Fisherman and the Goblet (A Vietnamese Folk Tale)*. Illustrated by Taro Yashima. San Carlos, Calif.: Golden Gate Junior Books, 1971.

Towle, Faith M. *The Magic Cooking Pot (A Folktale of India)*. Boston: Houghton Mifflin, 1975.

Yolen, Jane, ed. *Favorite Folktales from Around the World*. New York: Pantheon, 1986.

Ghost Stories

Adler, C. S. *Footsteps on the Stairs*. New York: Delacorte, 1982. (Ages 11-up)

Brittain, Bill. *Who Knew There'd Be Ghosts?* Illustrated by Michele Chessare. New York: Harper and Row, 1985. (Ages 8-11)

Butler, Beverly. *Ghost Cat*. New York: Dodd, Mead, 1984. (Ages 10-up)

Colby, C. B. *World's Best "True" Ghost Stories*. New York: Sterling, 1988.

Hahn, Mary Downing. *Wait Till Helen Comes: A Ghost Story*. Boston: Clarion, 1986. (Ages 8-12)

Martin, Bill, Jr., and John Archambault. *The Ghost-Eye Tree*. Illustrated by Ted Rand. New York: Holt, Rinehart and Winston, 1985.

San Souci, Robert D. *Thirty Chilling Tales Short and Shivery*. Illustrated by Katherine Coville. New York: Doubleday, 1987.

Schwartz, Alvin. *Scary Stories to Tell in the Dark*. Drawings by Stephen Gammell. New York: Harper and Row, 1981.

_____. *More Scary Stories to Tell in the Dark*. Drawings by Stephen Gammell. New York: Harper and Row, 1984.

Wright, Betty Ren. *Christina's Ghost*. New York: Holiday House, 1985. (Ages 8-11)

How and Why Tales

Bowden, Joan Chase. *Why the Tides Ebb and Flow*. Illustrated by Marc Brown. Boston: Houghton Mifflin, 1979.

Connolly, James E. *Why the Possum's Tail Is Bare (and Other North American Indian Nature Tales)*. Illustrated by Andrea Adams. Owings Mills, Md.: Stemmer House, 1975.

Dayrell, Elphinstone. *Why the Sun and the Moon Live in the Sky (An African Folktale)*. Illustrated by Blair Lent. Boston: Houghton Mifflin, 1968.

Kipling, Rudyard. *How the Camel Got His Hump*. Illustrated by Tim Raglin. Saxonville, Md.: Rabbit Ears, 1990. Cassette: Narrated by Danny Glover, music by Ladysmith Black Mambazo.

_____. *Just So Stories*. New York: Weathervane, 1978.

Legends

Cohen, Caron Lee. *The Mud Pony: A Traditional Skidi Pawnee Tale*. Illustrated by Shonto Begay. New York: Scholastic/Hardcover Books, 1988. (Ages 4-8; picture book)

Connolly, James. *Why the Possum's Tail Is Bare, and Other Northern American Indian Nature Tales*. Illustrated by Andrea Adams. Owings Mill, Md.: Stemmer House, 1985. (Ages 7-12)

Cooper, Susan. *The Selkie Girl*. Illustrated by Warwick Hutton. New York: McElderry, 1986. (Ages 8-11)

Curry, Jane Louise. *Back in the Beforetime: Tales of the California Indians*. Illustrated by James Watts. New York: McElderry, 1987. (Ages 9-12)

dePaola, Tomie. *The Legend of the Bluebonnet*. Illustrated by author. New York: Putnam, 1983.

_____. *The Legend of the Indian Paintbrush*. Illustrated by author. New York: Putnam, 1988. (Ages 4-8; picture book)

_____. *The Legend of Old Befana*. Illustrated by author. New York: Harcourt Brace Jovanovich, 1980.

deWit, Dorothy, ed. *The Talking Stone*. New York: Greenwillow, 1979.

Erdoes, Richard, and Alfonso Ortiz, selectors and eds. *American Indian Myths and Legends*. New York: Pantheon, 1984.

Goble, Paul. *Her Seven Brothers*. Illustrated by author. New York: Bradbury, 1988. (Ages 5-9; picture book)

_____. *Iktomi and the Boulder: A Plains Indian Story*. Illustrated by author. Orchard, 1988. (Ages 6-10)

Grant, Niel. *American Folk Tales and Legends*. London: Octopus, 1988.

Hastings, Selina. *Sir Gawain and the Loathly Lady*. Illustrated by Juan Wijngaard. New York: Lothrop, Lee and Shepard, 1985. (Ages 9-12)

Heyer, Marilee. *The Weaving of a Dream: A Chinese Folktale*. Illustrated by author. New York: Viking-Kestrel, 1986. (Ages 8-10)

Mayer, Mercer. *The Pied Piper of Hamelin*. Illustrated by author. New York: Macmillan, 1987. (Ages 6-10; picture book)

Mayo, Gretchen Will. *Star Tales: North American Indian Stories about the Stars*. Illustrated by author. New York: Walker, 1987. (Ages 8-12)

Osborne, Will, and Mary Pope Osborne. *Jason and the Argonauts*. Illustrated by Steven Sullivan. New York: Scholastic, 1988. (Ages 10-12)

Philip, Neil. *The Tale of Sir Gawain*. Illustrated by Charles Keeping. New York: Philomel, 1987. (Ages 9-12)

South Dakota Writers' Project, comp. *Legends of the Mighty Sioux*. Illustrated by Oscar Howe. Interior, SD: Badlands Natural History Association, 1987.

Myths

Baskin, Hosie, and Leonard Baskin. *A Book of Dragons*. Illustrated by Leonard Baskin. New York: Knopf/Borzoi, 1985. (Ages 9-12)

Campbell, Joseph. *The Power of Myths*. New York: Bantam Doubleday Dell, 1988.

Climo, Shirley. *King of the Birds*. Illustrated by Ruth Heller. New York: Crowell, 1988. (Ages 4-7; picture book)

d'Aulaire, Ingri, and Edgar d'Aulaire. *Book of Greek Myths*. New York: Bantam Doubleday Dell, 1962.

Gerstein, Mordicai. *Tales of Pan*. Illustrated by author. New York: Harper and Row, 1986. (Ages 9-12; picture book)

Giddings, Ruth Warner. *Yaqui Myths and Legends*. Illustrated by Laurie Cook. Tucson: University of Arizona Press, 1983.

Goble, Paul. *The Great Race of the Birds and Animals*. Illustrated by author. New York: Bradbury, 1985. (Ages 6-10; picture book)

Hamilton, Virginia. *In the Beginning*. Illustrated by Barry Moser. New York: Harcourt Brace Jovanovich, 1988.

Lattimore, Deborah N. *The Prince and the Golden Ax: A Minoan Tale*. Illustrated by author. New York: Harper and Row, 1988. (Ages 4-8; picture book)

Low, Alice. *The Macmillan Book of Greek Gods and Heros*. Illustrated by Arvis Stewart. New York: Macmillan, 1985.

Monroe, Jean G., and Ray Williamson. *They Dance in the Sky: Native American Star Myths*. Illustrated by Edgar Stewart. New York: Houghton Mifflin, 1987. (Ages 10-up)

Osborne, Mary Pope. *Pandora's Box*. Illustrated by Lasa Amoroso. New York: Scholastic/Hello Reader Books, 1987. (Ages 5-9; picture book)

Weil, Lisl. *Pandora's Box*. Illustrated by author. New York: Atheneum, 1986. (Ages 7-10; picture book)

Tall Tales

Aylesworth, Jim. *Shenandoah Noah*. Illustrated by Glen Rounds. New York: Holt, Rinehart and Winston, 1985.

Cohen, Caron Lee. *Sally Ann Thunder and Whirlwind Crockett*. Illustrated by Ariane Dewey. New York: Greenwillow, 1985.

Dewey, Ariane. *Febold Feboldson*. New York: Greenwillow, 1984.

_____. *Laffite the Pirate*. New York: Greenwillow, 1985.

Gleeson, Brian. *Pecos Bill*. Illustrated by Tim Raglin. Saxonville, Md.: Rabbit Ears, 1990.

Kellogg, Steven. *Johnny Appleseed: A Tall Tale*. New York: Morrow, 1988.

_____. *Paul Bunyan: The Tall Tale Retold*. New York: Morrow, 1984.

Noble, Trinka Hakes. *Meanwhile Back at the Ranch*. Illustrated by Tony Ross. New York: Dial, 1987.

O'Shea, Pat. *Finn Mack Cool and the Small Men of Deeds*. Illustrated by Stephen Lavis. Holiday House, 1987.

Schwartz, Alvin. *Whopper: Tall Tales and Other Lies Collected from American Folklore*. Illustrated by Glen Rounds. New York: Lippincott, 1975.

Stevenson, James. *That Dreadful Day*. New York: Greenwillow, 1985.

_____. *We Hate Rain!* New York: Greenwillow, 1988.

Talbott, Hudson. *We're Back! A Dinosaur's Story*. New York: Crown, 1987.

Urban Legends

Brunvand, Jan Harold. *The Choking Doberman*. New York: Norton, 1984.

_____. *Curses! Broiled Again!* New York: Norton, 1989.

_____. *The Mexican Pet*. New York: Norton, 1986.

_____. *The Vanishing Hitchhiker: American Urban Legends and Their Meanings*. New York: Norton, 1981.

Dickson, Paul, and Joseph C. Goulden. *There Are Alligators in Our Sewers and Other American Credos*. New York: Delacorte, 1983.

3 Taking Fact into Fiction

Mark Twain reportedly said, "It's a mighty poor storyteller that can't tell it better than it actually happened." In this chapter we will show students how they can take facts about a subject or an event and shape those facts into a good telling story by editing and finding detail that will bring the story to life. We will begin with the primary source for factual stories—the storytellers themselves.

GETTING THE REMEMBERED FACTS

Stories about Ourselves

Students may say they don't know any good stories about themselves. The following are activities that should help them get in touch with those stories.

► ACTIVITIES

MY LIFE STORY

Ask parents to spend an evening with their children showing them the photographs that were taken when the children were little. (Figure 3.1 shows a suggested letter to parents.) The students might ask:

- Where and when was the picture taken?

- How old was I when that picture was taken?

- What was important about the day that you took the picture?

- What was I like when I was that age?

- Who are the other people in the photograph?

- Why are they there?

- What do you remember about the day it was taken?

- What else of significance should I notice about the picture?

Parents could also show students old report cards, favorite objects, or previous work saved. From this "life history" students should select two or three incidents to tell about. Information on shaping the story for telling is included at the end of this section.

Dear Parent(s),

We'd like your help. As part of our whole language program, the children are working on skills related to oral language. The activity during the next week is "my life." The children will select two or three incidents from their life to tell about.

You can help your child "remember when." Would you spend an evening with your child showing him or her the photographs that were taken when he or she was little? You might share:

- Where and when was the picture taken?

- How old was the child when that picture was taken?

- What was important about the day that you took the picture?

- What was the child like when the child was that age?

- Who are the other people in the photograph?

- Why are they there?

- What do you remember about the day the picture was taken?

- What else of significance should your child notice about the picture?

You might also wish to share old report cards, favorite objects, or school papers that you've saved.

You and your child will have a special evening remembering when. I'm looking forward to hearing the stories. Thanks for your help.

Sincerely,

(Teacher's Name)

Fig. 3.1. Suggested letter to parents.

STORYTELLING JOURNAL

Have students keep a journal of events in their lives or the lives of others that might make good telling stories. They may wish to record unusual characters they see or meet, vivid descriptions they read or hear, unusual or catchy phrases they read or hear, and feelings they have experienced.

A SPECIAL MEMORY

In a small group the students can brainstorm story ideas from their pasts. Topics for discussion might include:

- The Hungriest I've Ever Been

- The Saddest I've Ever Been

- I Laughed 'Til I Almost Cried

- The Favorite Gift I've Received
- The Favorite Gift I've Given
- The Hardest Thing I've Had to Do
- A Trip I'll Never Forget
- My Most Frightening Experience
- A Special Christmas
- Holiday Customs of My Family
- My Most Embarrassing Moment

After the students have gotten in touch with their memories, have them shape the incidents into telling stories using details that will bring the stories to life.

MY YESTERDAY: STORYTELLING JOURNAL

The happenings of yesterday and today may be important material for storytelling. Have students remember three things or three scenes from their yesterday. Have them organize and write those for inclusion in their storytelling journal. Later students can review their journal and shape recorded incidents into telling stories. A teacher, Marilyn Simpson from Watford City, North Dakota, told her students about the "olden days"—the days before microwave ovens, VCRs, and paperback books. The students were fascinated and asked for more stories of the old days. Today's reality is tomorrow's history.

THAT REMINDS ME

The teacher collects a large quantity of old family photographs and spreads them out around the room. Students select a photograph that reminds them of something in their own life. Have the students move around the room and share with others the memory their chosen photograph evokes. That memory may be shaped into a telling story.

Family Stories

Families are rich sources of folklore. The demise of the close extended family has made it even more important that students collect tales from their older relatives before the stories are forgotten. As we share family memories we share what it means to be a family. We share our beliefs, our fears, our joys, our tragedies, our dreams, and our disappointments. The collecting and sharing of these tales will be a rich experience for both students and family members.

▶ ACTIVITIES

INTERVIEWING RELATIVES OR
OLDER MEMBERS OF THE COMMUNITY

Have students select an older relative or older person in the community to interview. The class may brainstorm questions they would like to ask, or they may use the interview sheet in figure 3.2. Students may either take notes or use a tape recorder. Parts of the interview may then be shaped into telling stories using the suggestions described later in the chapter. Two examples of family stories follow the interview sheet.

STORIES ABOUT PEOPLE WE KNOW:

INTERVIEW:

Talk to great grandparents or an older person in your community about:

Fads in their time _____

How grandpa and grandma met _____

_____

What radio programs they listened to _____

_____

What kind of music they listened to _____

A naughty thing they did _____

_____

The consequences of the naughty act (punishment) _____

_____

What school was like _____

_____

How they got to school _____

_____

Some popular phrases of their time _____

_____

What those phrases mean _____

_____

_____

STORYTELLING: Write or tell a story about one day in the life of Grandma or Grandpa.

Fig. 3.2. Interview sheet.

Mother and the Snake

Mary Helen Pelton

It is a bad combination. My husband, Ray, is quite a trickster and his mother is afraid of snakes. The family lived on a farm about eight miles from the nearest town. With six children and poor roads, mother Florence occasionally felt isolated and always looked forward to the arrival of the mail. Each day Ray walked down to the mail box to collect the newspaper and letters. As he approached the house his mom would rush outside to grab the parcel.

One day Ray purchased a toy snake at the local dime store and stuffed it in the center of the mail. His mom ran out of the house and grabbed the mail as usual. Out of the *Dickinson Press* popped a long, green, beady-eyed snake. Florence screamed, dropped the mail and grabbed a hoe. She hacked madly away at what appeared to be a writhing reptile. "Mom, stop, stop, it's just a rubber snake," pleaded Ray.

She didn't lose a beat as she flailed away, "rubber snake, rubber snake, what kind of a snake is a rubber snake?"

*Allergies**

Jackie DiGennaro

Because of an ear infection, my young son, Casey, had to go to the pediatrician. I was impressed with the way the doctor directed his comments and questions to my son. When he asked Casey, "Is there anything you are allergic to?" Casey nodded and whispered in his ear. Smiling, the pediatrician wrote out a prescription and handed it to me. Without looking at it, I tucked it into my purse.

Later, the pharmacist filled the order, remarking on the unusual food-drug interaction my son must have. When he saw my puzzled expression, he showed me the label on the bottle. As per the doctor's instructions, it read: "Do not take with broccoli."

THE STORY OF FAMILY TREASURES

Have students ask a relative or older citizen to tell the stories behind some of the treasures in his or her house, such as an old jewelry box, a tool chest filled with old woodworking tools, an old stamp box, or an antique vase. This story would also be effective told in the first person by the great, great grandmother. Have students use the information they gather in their interviews to create a telling story.

The Pendant

Mary Helen Pelton

My great aunt Kassie, a gracious southern lady from Atlanta, Georgia, gave me a pearl pendant that had been in our family since the mid 1800s. The pendant survived the Civil War through the ingenuity of our great, great grandmother. During Sherman's march to the sea, the armies destroyed much that was in their path, including most of our family possessions. The little pendant, along with a few other treasures, was saved, however. Grandma had hidden them in the garden in the roots of the pecan trees.

DIARIES, LETTERS, AND NEWSPAPER CLIPPINGS

Rich sources of family histories are old letters, diaries, and newspaper clippings. Fascinating family tales can be constructed from these sources. This story is reconstructed from letters and newspaper clippings two sisters found in the attic.

She Was So Young

Mary Helen Pelton

The two year old played at the feet of his pretty dark-haired mother. The sky outside grew dark and threatening. She closed the window against the impending rain.

She walked to the sofa, turned on the electric lamp, and sat down to read a love letter from her husband who was away on business. The little boy whimpered as the thunder shook the walls.

The rain that followed was somehow comforting. Yet the comfort was short-lived. As a fiery sword thrown by an angry God, the lightning struck the house and traveled through the wires. Like a deadly viper the lightning leaped out of the lamp and sunk its fangs into the young mother killing her instantly. My father's mother was only twenty-one—dead before her life had begun. And the two year old was left alone.

THE GREAT DISASTER

Asking family members or older citizens to remember natural disasters such as earthquakes, blizzards, floods, hurricanes, tornadoes, and droughts will often produce fascinating tales. If students are interviewing an older person who has lived his or her life in that community, the students may wish to prepare themselves for the interview by reviewing old newspapers available at the local newspaper office. They can incorporate what they already know about the subject into their interview and later combine their research with the personal account to create a memorable tale.

SHAPING THE EXPERIENCE INTO A TELLING STORY

The student must now weave fact and fiction. In the story "The Pendant," the author simply reported the facts in an interesting way. If, however, the author had chosen to write the story in the first person, she would have fictionalized the account, since she has no real way of knowing what great, great grandmother said or felt as she hid her treasures in the tree roots. At first this may be hard for students. They may feel that by editing or deleting, by adding detail or taking it out, they are in some sense lying to the listener. That can be easily remedied by having students say, "This is a tale based on a true story told to me by my grandmother." (Note the words "based on.") Students are not reporting an incident verbatim; rather they are weaving fact and fiction.

Shaping the story for telling involves several steps. In *Storyteller* (1972), Ramon Ross offers this advice:

1. The teller must identify the experiences to tell about.

2. The teller must give the story a time and place.

3. The teller must choose detail that brings the characters to life. The teller must show the characters, not tell about them.

4. The teller must cut and shape the story. Does the story have a strong beginning? Does the language of the story create visual images for the listener? Does it connect to the audience? Is unnecessary detail eliminated? Does it have a satisfactory conclusion?

5. The teller should record and practice the tale.

In *The National Storytelling Journal* (1989, 16-17), Donald Davis suggests incorporating the following elements into family stories: "1) a clear meeting with the main character as a three-dimensional and potentially changeable person living in a real world, 2) an event of crisis or wounding that turns established ways of relating to the world upside down, 3) a set of learnings or discoveries that are prompted by this particular crisis and that could have happened in no other way, and 4) the subsequent trial or application of what has been learned to see if it works in the whole world of greater life and reality" (1989, 16). Davis goes on to say that creating family stories is not like taking family pictures. As the teller we are the active interpreter, and from that comes "the true joy of helping long-forgotten people come to life, not only for those who loved them but also for those who never had a chance to know them" (1989, 17).

Newspapers

Newspapers can be excellent sources for stories. The story written below is an example of a story based on a newspaper article. First the author recorded the facts she wanted to include in the story. Then she went from fact to fiction.

Fact: Post-it™ Notes

- Invented in 1974 while Art Fry was sitting through a boring sermon.
- Nonsticking glue discovered by Spencer Silver.
- Both men are engineers at 3-M company.

Fiction:

I'm a Traveling Man

Mary Helen Pelton

I've been places you never thought of going. Can't remember who I am, huh? I'm a Post-it. Well, you'll recognize me in a minute. I'm everywhere. Think yellow. Think 3x5. Think stick but can be removed without ripping the paper. Recognize me now? (Show the audience the Post-it.)

I was born in 1974 when Art Fry was sitting through a boring church sermon. The markers in his choir book kept falling out. He thought, "Gee what I need is a bookmark that will stick to the pages lightly. I'd need to take them off after the church service without damaging the book."

A few years before, Spencer Silver, another scientist at 3-M, had accidentally invented a glue that was strong enough to hold paper but could be easily removed. No one liked it though. I mean who wants a glue that doesn't stick? My buddy Art did!

Art cut out a piece of paper, put some glue on it, stuck the pages together in a little tablet, and BINGO!! I was invented. Now you'll find me or one of my cousins everywhere. We come in all shapes, sizes, and colors. Like I said before, I'm a traveling man. You'll find me everywhere:

- Sticking to the refrigerator to remind the kids what they are supposed to do after school

- Moving from report to report carrying important messages from person to person in every office in the USA and probably the world

- Carrying love notes to sweethearts on windows of cars

- Reminding people of things they need to do that day (my favorite place for that is on bathroom mirrors)

I come in a new variety now—Post-its with little messages already printed on them. For example, a little girl got a package of Post-its from her brother, Fred, with "Have a nice day somewhere else" printed on it. She posted them all over the house with notes that said, Dear Fred, "See message above" from the monster of the deep, or the hairy toad, or your sister who doesn't want to be in this family if you're in it.

In case you're wondering, I can also still be found in a church hymnal. A fellow never wants to get too far from his roots.

► **ACTIVITY**

GUESS WHAT HAPPENED TODAY

Have students keep a file on interesting newspaper articles that can later be turned into telling stories. In my file, for example, are stories about:

- A docile dog who saved the life of her owner during an armed robbery

- A rare, bright-blue lobster found in only one in four million catches

- People who swallow their tooth brushes

- A Canadian and Soviet team who skied across the North Pole

- Henry, a wild turkey, who escorts people throughout the town in Medina, North Dakota (he even tried to go to church one day)

- Parachutists who are trying to block the government wolf kill in British Columbia

- A man who kidnapped a pair of 3½-ton elephants and kept them hidden for four years

- Two dogs who led their owner to a truck driver pinned beneath a 2,600-pound farm implement tire (the temperature was twenty degrees below zero that night)

- A wild moose who was so in love with a cow that he courted her for months

Since news articles are usually crisp and concise, they are useful for extemporaneous telling. Have students in small groups read a newspaper story and retell the story with only five minutes preparation.

Research on Person, Place, Object

Students will learn valuable research skills as well as the use of active imagination by incorporating factual material gathered from research into the stories they create.

Students may use the research sheets shown in figures 3.3, 3.4, and 3.5 to gather facts about an object, person, or place; or they can create their own note-gathering format.

► **ACTIVITY**

MORE THAN THE FACTS

Students collect enough factual material about an object, person, or place to weave an interesting tale about the subject researched. They then combine fact and fiction bringing material to life for oral retelling. Students may wish to assume the first person when creating a tale about a person or object.

(Text continues on page 64.)

CREATE A STORY FROM RESEARCH: OBJECT

Choose an object that you would like to research, such as a favorite object or a specific kind of rock, tree, food, or tool. Then prepare a fictional story about the object.

1. What is the object you chose? _____

2. Where is the object located? _____

    _____

3. When did you see it? _____

    _____

4. Describe the object so that the listener can visualize it. _____

    _____

    _____

    _____

    _____

5. How is the object used by people? _____

    _____

    _____

    _____

    _____

6. What is there about the object that you find particularly interesting? _____

    _____

    _____

    _____

(If you need more writing space, use the back of this sheet or a separate sheet of paper.)

Fig. 3.3.

CREATE A STORY FROM RESEARCH: PLACE

Choose a place that you would like to research, such as a place of interest in a specific city, state, or country. Then prepare a story about an imaginary trip that you took to this place. Practice the story before you tell it to your classmates.

1. Where in the world did you go? _____

2. When did you go? _____

3. How did you go? _____

_____

4. Why did you go there? _____

_____

_____

_____

_____

5. What did you do there? (You might describe what you saw, heard, smelled, tasted, and touched as well as what you did there.) _____

_____

_____

_____

_____

_____

_____

_____

_____

(If you need more writing space, use the back of this sheet or a separate sheet of paper.)

Fig. 3.4.

CREATE A STORY FROM RESEARCH: PERSON

Choose a famous person to research, such as a person in history, sports, science, literature, art, or music. Then prepare a story about this person. You might even pretend that you are this person when you tell the story.

1. Where and when was this person born? Where did this person live as a child and as an adult? _____

_____

2. What did this person do to become famous? _____

_____

_____

_____

_____

3. What other interesting facts about this person would you like to include in your story? _____

_____

_____

_____

_____

_____

4. What do you admire about this person? Why? _____

_____

_____

_____

_____

(If you need more writing space, use the back of this sheet or a separate sheet of paper.)

Fig. 3.5.

►ACTIVITIES

The following is an example of a story from Abraham Lincoln's life.

Facts: Abraham Lincoln

- He was the sixteenth president of the United States.

- In early April 1865, he had a bad dream in which he saw himself lying in state in the East Room of the White House, killed by an assassin's bullet.

- On April 14, 1865, while attending the Ford Theater with his wife, Mary, he was shot by John Wilkes Booth; he died the next day.

- His body lay in state in the East Room of the White House where thousands of people mourned him.

A Nation Mourns

Mary Helen Pelton

Are nightmares just horror movies of the mind, or do they show us frightening glimpses into our future? Abraham Lincoln, the sixteenth president of the United States, had such a dream. Did it project the future? I'll let you decide the answer to that question after you hear President Lincoln's story. (Storytellers note: Mr. Lincoln speaks.)

"During the great Civil War my friends worried about my safety. Guess some of my enemies thought they could save the confederacy if they assassinated the president. I'd be less than honest if I told you that it didn't worry me. I had haunting dreams.

I'll never forget the terrifying dream I had in April, right before the fall of the confederacy. I dreamed that I was wandering through the White House. My footsteps echoed through the empty halls. Why was no one there? Where were the guards? The servants? Then I heard it. But what was it? A dog whimpering? A hurt child? As I drew closer to the East Room of the White House, the noise became louder and more distinct. What horror waited me as I entered there! In the center of the room lay a corpse dressed in a dark shroud, and about the corpse was a throng of people weeping piteously. I moved closer to see the face but was stopped by the guards surrounding the corpse. 'Who is it that these people mourn?' I asked of one of the guards. 'Why, haven't you heard?' answered the guard incredulously. 'The President of the United States has been killed by an assassin's bullet.'

"A woman screamed, the crowd wailed.... I awoke and slept no more that night."

On April 14, 1865, Mr. Lincoln and his wife, Mary, attended the Ford Theater, where *Our American Cousin* was playing. During the third act, a shadowy figure stepped into the theater box and shot Mr. Lincoln. Although five doctors worked on the president all night, he died at 7:22 a.m. on April 15. The funeral was held in the East Room of the White House four days later. As the body of the fallen president lay in state surrounded by guards, thousands of people filed past his coffin weeping piteously.

Just a nightmare, or a glimpse into the future?

STORY ABOUT AN INTRIGUING CAREER

Students can also weave tales about people in their own lives. Using an interview sheets like the one in figure 3.6, students might interview people in the community about their lives and careers. One person is invited into the classroom so that the teacher can "model" the interview process. Have students create a story, either fact or fiction, using the information gained in the interview.

Interview:

Invite someone from an occupation that interests you and ask questions like these:

What is your major job responsibility? _____

What other important responsibilities do you have that not many people know about? _____

_____

Why did you want to be a (_____)? _____

What advice would you give to a kid who wants to be a (_____)? _____

_____

What is a typical day for you? _____

Fig. 3.6.

► ACTIVITY

STORY FROM SCIENTIFIC FACT

Students research a scientific fact and then create a story based on those facts. Some suggestions are:

- How hail comes to be
- What causes the northern lights
- Journey of salmon to spawn
- Caterpillars' growth into butterflies
- History of a snowflake
- Changing of the tides
- Eclipse of the sun
- How paper comes from trees
- What causes popcorn to pop

CONCLUSION

Weaving fact and fiction has many advantages:

- It provides rich source material for students to work from while still encouraging their creative imaginations.
- It puts students in touch with their own stories.
- It puts students in touch with the lives of their families.
- It encourages newspaper reading.
- It encourages research.
- It helps students be more discriminating readers and listeners as they develop a greater understanding of fact and fiction.

BIBLIOGRAPHY

Arthur, Stephen, and Julia Arthur. *Your Life and Times: How to Put a Life Story on Tape—An Oral History Handbook*. Nobleton, Fla.: Heritage Tree, 1986.

Baum, Willa K. *Transcribing and Editing Oral History*. Nashville: American Association for State and Local History, 1977.

Bosma, Bette. *Fairy Tales, Fables, Legends and Myths*. New York: Teachers College Press, 1987.

Davis, Cullom, Kathryn Back, and Kay MacLean. *Oral History from Tape to Type*. Chicago: American Library Association, 1977.

Davis, Donald D. "Creating Family Stories." *National Storytelling Journal* (Fall 1989), 16-17.

Dorson, Richard M., ed. *Handbook of American Folklore*. Bloomington: Indiana University Press, 1986.

Hoopes, James. *Oral History: An Introduction for Students*. Chapel Hill: University of North Carolina Press, 1979.

Kinghorn, Harriet, and Mary Morberg. *Research Shapes: Animals*. Illustrated by Susan Cronin-Paris. Palo Alto, Calif.: Monday Morning Books, distributed by Good Apple, 1989.

_____. *Research Shapes: Inventions*. Illustrated by Susan Cronin-Paris. Palo Alto, Calif.: Monday Morning Books, distributed by Good Apple, 1989.

_____. *Research Shapes: Transportation*. Illustrated by Susan Cronin-Paris. Palo Alto, Calif.: Monday Morning Books, distributed by Good Apple, 1989.

Ross, Ramon. *Storyteller*, 2d ed. Columbus, Ohio: Merrill, 1972.

Sitton, Thad, George L. Mehaffy, and O. L. Davis, Jr. *Oral History: A Guide for Teachers (and Others)*. Austin: University of Texas Press, 1983.

Wigginton, Eliot. *Sometimes a Shining Moment: The Foxfire Experience*. Garden City, N.Y.: Anchor, 1986.

Zeitlin, Steven J., Amy J. Kotkin, and Holly Cutting Baker. *A Celebration of American Family Folklore*. New York: Pantheon, 1982.

4 Readers Theatre

Open the curtain and let the performance begin. Readers theatre is not a play. There are no sets, no costumes, no memorized lines. Readers theatre is an interpretative reading, giving children a chance to bring their characters to life through voice and gesture while feeling "safe" with a text in hand. While the performers entertain with dramatic reading style, the listeners create their own vivid mental image of the story.

Teachers and students can write their own materials using folk literature, stories, poems, and real-life experience. It's simple. Have the character speak as much as possible—even if the character is thinking out loud. Try to limit the number of characters so that your audience doesn't get confused with who is who. Give most of the dialogue to the characters—if the narrator dominates a scene, the audience may lose interest.

As in all good telling stories the scripts should have:

- Emotional appeal

- Dramatic conflict

- Unique characters who react strongly (the audience should be able to "see" the characters)

- Good figurative language and strong sensory images

In the beginning, the narrator will introduce the characters and the performers. The characters should address each other by name until identities are clearly established. To add interest to the stage, the performers may sit on platforms, stools, chairs, ladders, or benches. The main character will be placed in the center with the other players grouped around that character. Groupings are much more interesting than students lined up across the stage.

As the performance begins, the readers focus their attention on the audience and not on the interaction among the characters. This helps the audience focus on the text rather than on the performers.

In the pages that follow the reader will find four examples of readers theatre. The first is based on an original story written by the fourth graders in Jackie DiGennaro's class in Sitka, Alaska. The second is a script developed from the folktale "Jack and the Beanstalk," written by Mary Helen Pelton. The last two selections are examples from *Readers Theatre for Young Adults* and *Readers Theatre for Children* by Kathy Latrobe and Mildred Laughlin. Now let the theatre begin.

The Candy Cane Reindeer

Jackie DiGennaro and her fourth-grade class

[This is a patterned story based on "The Gingerbread Boy." First the author presents the story, then shows how she changed it into a readers theatre script.]

Once upon a time, far away at the North Pole, Mrs. Santa was in her kitchen cooking up a little surprise for Santa Claus. She mixed a little sugar, a little spice, and a pinch of goodness and stirred it all up in a big pot. Then she rolled it and shaped it into a candy cane reindeer.

When Mrs. Claus was finished, the candy cane reindeer jumped up and shouted, "I'm a candy cane reindeer, I'm as sweet as can be. I can fly so fast, you can't catch me!"

With that, the candy cane reindeer flew out of the kitchen and into the den where Santa was dozing in his armchair.

Santa awoke with a start. "Oh, ho!" He exclaimed. "Stop, little reindeer! I want to eat you!"

But the candy cane reindeer replied, "I'm a candy cane reindeer. I'm as sweet as can be. I can fly so fast, you can't catch me! I flew away from Mrs. Claus just as fast as could be, and I'll fly away from you—just you wait and see."

And with those words, the little reindeer flew out of the den with Santa and Mrs. Claus following close behind.

By and by the little reindeer came to Santa's workshop where the elves were busily hammering, sawing, and working away on toys for Christmas. When they spotted the reindeer, they all shouted "Stop! We want to eat you!"

But the candy cane reindeer only laughed and replied, "I'm a candy cane reindeer. I'm as sweet as can be. I can fly so fast, you can't catch me—I flew away from Santa and Mrs. Claus just as fast as could be, and I'll fly away from you—just you wait and see!"

With those words, the little reindeer laughed and flew out of the workshop, with the elves, Santa, and Mrs. Claus following close behind.

By and by the candy cane reindeer came to the stable, where Rudolph was polishing Santa's sleighbells in preparation for Christmas Eve. When Rudolph spied the little reindeer, he cried, "Stop! I want to eat you!"

But the candy cane reindeer only laughed and replied, "I'm a candy cane reindeer. I'm as sweet as can be. I can fly so fast, you can't catch me! I flew away from Santa and Mrs. Claus and the elves just as fast as could be and I'll fly away from you—just you wait and see!"

With that the little reindeer flew out of the stable and into the snow, with Rudolph, the elves, Santa, and Mrs. Claus following close behind.

By and by the candy cane reindeer chanced upon Frosty the Snowman, frolicking in the snow. When Frosty spotted the little reindeer he shouted, "Stop, little reindeer! I want to eat you!"

But the candy cane reindeer only laughed at Frosty and answered, "I'm a candy cane reindeer. I'm as sweet as can be. I can fly so fast, you can't catch me. I flew away from Rudolph, the elves, Santa and Mrs. Claus, just as fast as could be, and I'll fly away from you—just you wait and see!"

With that the little reindeer flew away into the snowy day, with Frosty, Rudolph, the elves, Santa, and Mrs. Claus following close behind.

After a short while the candy cane reindeer started feeling cold. Spying an inviting-looking house with smoke curling from the chimney, he ducked down the chimney and into the living room of the cozy little house. Hanging in front of the fireplace was a beautiful red and white stocking with the name "Amy" embroidered on it in green thread. "I'll just hop in here for a quick nap," thought the reindeer to himself as he snuggled into the toe of the stocking.

When the little reindeer awoke, he could not move, for he was wedged in between an orange and a large baby doll with big blue eyes. He felt himself lifted through the air and heard the squeals of a little girl as she exclaimed, "A candy cane reindeer! How yummy!"

And before you could say "Merry Christmas," crunch and munch, the little candy cane reindeer was gobbled up, which, after all, is what he was made for in the first place.

THE CANDY CANE REINDEER
Readers Theatre

NARRATOR: The readers theatre we will present today is based on an original story written by Jackie DiGennaro's fourth-grade class. The characters in our play are Mrs. Claus, read by _____; Santa, read by _____; Elves, read by _____, _____, and _____; Rudolph, read by _____; Frosty, read by _____; and a little girl named Amy, read by _____. I, _____, will be your narrator.

Once upon a time, far away at the North Pole, Mrs. Santa was in her kitchen cooking up a little surprise for Santa Claus. She mixed a little sugar, a little spice, and a pinch of goodness and stirred it all up in a big pot. Then she rolled it and shaped it into a candy cane reindeer. When Mrs. Claus was finished, the candy cane reindeer jumped up.

CANDY CANE REINDEER: I'm a candy cane reindeer, I'm as sweet as can be. I can fly so fast, you can't catch me!

NARRATOR: With that, the candy cane reindeer flew out of the kitchen and into the den where Santa was dozing in his armchair. He awoke with a start.

SANTA: Oh, ho! Stop, little reindeer! I want to eat you!

CANDY CANE REINDEER: I'm a candy cane reindeer, I'm as sweet as can be. I can fly so fast, you can't catch me! I flew away from Mrs. Claus just as fast as could be, and I'll fly away from you—just you wait and see.

NARRATOR: And with those words, the little reindeer flew out of the den with Santa and Mrs. Claus following close behind. By and by, the little reindeer came to Santa's workshop where the elves were busily hammering, sawing, and working away on toys for Christmas. They spotted the reindeer and all began chasing him.

ELVES: Stop! We want to eat you!

CANDY CANE REINDEER: I'm a candy cane reindeer. I'm as sweet as can be. I can fly so fast, you can't catch me! I flew away from Santa and Mrs. Claus just as fast as could be, and I'll fly away from you—just you wait and see!

NARRATOR: With those words, the little reindeer laughed and flew out of the workshop, with the elves, Santa, and Mrs. Claus following close behind. By and by the candy cane reindeer came to the stable, where Rudolph was polishing Santa's sleighbells in preparation for Christmas Eve. When Rudolph spied the little reindeer, he started chasing him, too.

RUDOLPH:	Stop! I want to eat you!
CANDY CANE REINDEER:	I'm a candy cane reindeer. I'm as sweet as can be. I can fly so fast, you can't catch me! I flew away from Santa and Mrs. Claus, and the elves just as fast as could be, and I'll fly away from you—just you wait and see!
NARRATOR:	With that, the little reindeer flew out of the stable and into the snow, with Rudolph, the elves, Santa and Mrs. Claus following close behind. By and by the candy cane reindeer chanced upon Frosty the Snowman, frolicking in the snow. When Frosty spotted the little reindeer he began chasing him.
FROSTY:	Stop, little reindeer! I want to eat you!
CANDY CANE REINDEER:	I'm a candy cane reindeer. I'm as sweet as can be. I can fly so fast, you can't catch me! I flew away from Rudolph, the elves, Santa and Mrs. Claus, just as fast as could be, and I'll fly away from you—just you wait and see!
NARRATOR:	With that the candy cane reindeer flew away into the snowy day, with Frosty, Rudolph, the elves, Santa, and Mrs. Claus following close behind. After a short while the candy cane reindeer started feeling cold. Spying an inviting-looking house with smoke curling from the chimney, he ducked down the chimney and into the living room of the cozy little house.
CANDY CANE REINDEER:	Oh, look! A row of pretty stockings hanging in front of the fireplace! I'll just jump into this one with "Amy" written on the top, and take a short nap.
NARRATOR:	So the reindeer snuggled into the toe of the stocking and fell fast asleep. But when he awoke, he could not move, for he was wedged in between an orange and a large baby doll with big blue eyes. Suddenly he felt himself being lifted through the air by a little girl.
AMY:	Oh, goodie! A candy cane reindeer! How yummy!
NARRATOR:	Before you could say "Merry Christmas," crunch and munch, the little candy cane reindeer was gobbled up, which, after all, is what he was made for in the first place.

Make a Candy Cane Reindeer:

Materials: Candy canes, small pom-poms and movable eyes (both available at craft stores), pipe cleaners. Optional: hot glue gun.

Method: Glue pom-pom on the curved end of the candy cane. Glue eyes in place. Cut pipe cleaner in half; twist into antler shape on top of candy cane.

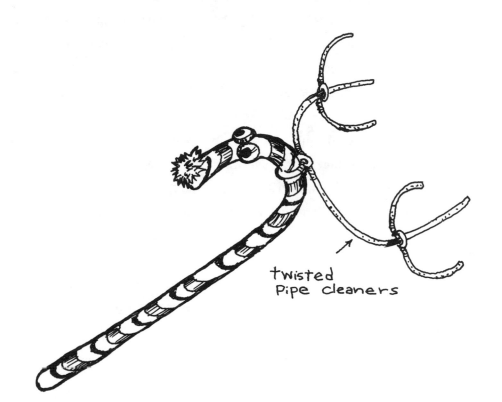

twisted
pipe cleaners

JACK AND THE BEANSTALK
Readers Theatre
Mary Helen Pelton

NARRATOR:	Today we will present a readers theatre based on the old folk tale "Jack and the Beanstalk." The characters are Jack, a boy who at times appears dim-witted, read by _____; his mother, a poor widow, read by _____; character on the road, read by _____; a wicked giant, read by _____; his wife, read by _____; Hen read by _____; and a beautiful harp, read by _____. I, _____, will be your narrator.
	In a time of magic and monsters, in a place across the sea, a boy named Jack lived in a simple cottage with his mother. Alas, they lived alone, for the father had long ago been killed by a horrible giant. One day the mother said:
MOTHER:	Jack, we have no food and no money for food. In two days we will starve. What shall we do?
JACK:	We could sell my clothes.
MOTHER:	That is sweet of you; however, the money from the sale of two pairs of worn britches and a well-mended shirt would not feed us even for a day.
JACK:	We could eat the cow.
MOTHER:	Oh dear me, that dear cow has been with us since you were a baby. I couldn't bear to eat it.
JACK:	Perhaps we could sell her then?
MOTHER:	What a brilliant idea, my son! Yes, take her to town immediately and sell her to a good family for the best price possible.
NARRATOR:	Jack took the cow up the winding road. He walked for half a day, and as he neared the market place he saw a shifty-looking fellow lounging beside the road.
CHARACTER:	Where are you going with that fine-looking cow, young man?
JACK:	I'm going to sell the cow to a fine family for a good price, sir.
CHARACTER:	How much do you want for her?
JACK:	At least $300.
CHARACTER:	Have I got a deal for you. I have something in my pocket which is worth not $100, not $200, not $300, but has a worth beyond man's and woman's imagination.
JACK:	Could I see this priceless thing?
CHARACTER:	Come step into the shadows with me, for robbers are about. Let me reach into my pocket. But remember you must not touch. Here ... see....
JACK:	But sir, I see only some colored beans.

CHARACTER:	To the common man's eye these are nothing but colored beans. However, in reality they are MAGIC beans ... possessing great power.
JACK:	If only I could own magic beans like these.
CHARACTER:	That could be arranged; perhaps we could trade the magic beans for your cow.
JACK:	You mean you'd trade your beans for this cow?
CHARACTER:	Certainly, consider it done.
NARRATOR:	And before Jack could reconsider, the man thrust the beans into Jack's hand and rapidly disappeared down the road leading his new cow.
JACK:	I can't believe my good fortune—mother will be so pleased.
NARRATOR:	But mother was not pleased.
MOTHER:	What do you mean you traded the cow for magic beans? Jack, you foolish boy, now we will certainly starve! These beans are good for nothing.
NARRATOR:	Out the window they went. Jack and his mother went to sleep cold—for there was no money for wood—and hungry—for there was no money for bread. Jack awoke early and went out to find the beans. He saw a miraculous sight.
JACK:	Look at the beanstalk! Why the stalk is thicker than my waist, the leaf stems are stronger than an iron ladder, and the height—I can't even see the top. It must go to heaven itself.
NARRATOR:	Jack grabbed the stalk and started his climb. After climbing for hours, he reached the top of the stalk and found himself in a land beyond our land.
JACK:	How strange! The trees are twice the normal size and the road ahead looks wide enough for an army. The ruts where a wagon has passed are taller than me.
NARRATOR:	A normal boy might have climbed down the beanstalk immediately, but Jack followed the road.
JACK:	Look at the castle! Why it's twice the size of the castle of our king. I wonder who lives there. I'll knock on the door and find out.
NARRATOR:	The most enormous woman Jack had ever seen appeared at the door. She was so big and Jack was so little she didn't even see him at first.
GIANT WOMAN:	Well, who's there!! Who knocks like a mouse at my door?
JACK:	I, good woman! I'm very hungry for I've traveled a long distance. May I trouble you for supper.
GIANT WOMAN:	You are an Englishman! It is dangerous for you! My husband the giant loves nothing better than to eat Englishmen, puny though you may be. But I am tender-hearted. Come in and I'll feed you.
NARRATOR:	Jack perched delicately on an enormous table and ate his fill. Suddenly the earth started to rumble and the table upon which Jack sat began to shake.

GIANT WOMAN:	Oh no!! My husband the giant is on his way home. He will be furious that I let a stranger in. Quickly, into this cupboard—you must hide at once.
GIANT:	Fie Fi Fo Fum I smell the blood of an Englishman Be he alive or be he dead I'll grind his bones to make my bread. Bring the Englishman to me, wife, for I long for a tasty morsel.
GIANT WOMAN:	Oh no, sir, there is no Englishman here—you smell the blood of the lamb I'm cooking for dinner.
GIANT:	Then let me eat the fatted lamb, and when I'm done bring me my bags of gold so I can count my money.
NARRATOR:	After dinner the giant wiped the dripping grease from his beard and counted his money. Soon he was sleeping soundly.
GIANT:	Zz Zz Zz
JACK:	Maybe I can crawl out of this cupboard and take the gold home to my dear mother.
NARRATOR:	And that's just what Jack did. While the giant was sleeping he took three large sacks of gold and crept silently out of the chamberhall and stole away down the beanstalk. He found his mother crying in their cottage.
MOTHER:	Oh, Jack, I thought something terrible had happened to you and I'd never see you again.
NARRATOR:	Jack told her the story of the giant and gave her the gold. They lived contentedly for a time, but one day Jack climbed the beanstalk and returned to the land of the giant. Again he knocked on the door of the giant and the giant's nearsighted wife answered.
JACK:	Please dear lady, I have been traveling a long, long way and am very hungry. Would you give me food?
GIANT WOMAN:	Oh dear me, no!! The last Englishman that was here stole my husband's gold. Besides, it is not safe for you here because my husband is most fond of eating Englishmen.
NARRATOR:	But Jack begged and pleaded 'til the kindhearted woman took him in and fed him scraps from lunch. The earth began to rumble and shake.
GIANT WOMAN:	Oh dear, the giant comes. Hide quickly under the bucket
GIANT:	Fie Fi Fo Fum I smell the blood of an Englishman Be he alive or be he dead I'll grind his bones to make my bread. Wife, bring me the Englishman at once—I'll eat him raw.

GIANT WOMAN:	No no, dear husband, there is no Englishman here—you smell the goat that I have in the stew pot.
GIANT:	Then bring it to me at once for I am powerfully hungry, then get my favorite pet, my hen that lays golden eggs, so she can perform for me.
GIANT WOMAN:	Here is your supper and your hen.
GIANT:	Look at how obedient she is—lay my pet.
HEN:	Cluck, Cluck, yes, master!
NARRATOR:	Egg after golden egg popped out from under the hen. One rolled directly to the place where Jack was hidden. He couldn't believe his eyes. After a time the giant became sleepy and began snoring loudly with his head on the table. Jack crept out from his hiding place, grabbed the hen, and ran for the beanstalk. He returned home safely with the hen but his mother said....
MOTHER:	Son, you must never go back up the beanstalk again. With this hen that lays golden eggs we have money to last for our lifetime. And surely if you return, the giant will kill you as he did your father. Please, never go again.
NARRATOR:	Jack tried to do as his mother requested, but the magic of the beanstalk and the power of the land beyond drew him to ascend once again. He again knocked at the door of the giant.
GIANT WOMAN:	You!! Another Englishman!! Go away at once. My husband will grind you and have you for supper.
JACK:	Please, just let me rest here a moment and I'll be on my way. Listen to the thunder and feel the rumble of the earth. A storm must be coming.
GIANT WOMAN:	Indeed, the storm is my husband. Hide quickly.
GIANT:	Fie Fi Fo Fum
	I smell the blood of an Englishman
	Be he alive or be he dead
	I'll grind his bones to make my bread.
	Where is the Englishman? Bring him to me at once!! I'll make a snack of him before supper.
GIANT WOMAN:	There is no Englishman here, husband. It is your imagination. You smell the beef burning on the grill.
GIANT:	Very well, bring it to me and bring my singing harp as well.
NARRATOR:	The giant ate his fill and commanded the harp to sing to him. As the harp sang sweet and gentle songs, the giant began to nod off and snore. Jack crept slowly out of his hiding place, grabbed the harp, and ran for the door.
HARP:	Master, master—help, master! I'm being taken!

GIANT:	What's that? Who called to me? A wretched boy has my harp. Come back you! You stole my gold and my hen, too. I'll squash you like an ant.
JACK:	I don't have much of a head start. I'd better run as I never have before.
HARP:	Help, master, help me!!
GIANT:	(Puffing) I'll squash you, you puny insect! Wait 'til I get my hands on you.
HARP:	Help, master, help!!
NARRATOR:	The giant was slow and clumsy. Jack ran like the wind. He got to the beanstalk, threw the harp over his shoulder, and began scrambling down. To his horror he looked up and saw that the giant was climbing down after him. When he got to the bottom, he called to his mother.
JACK:	Mother, quickly bring me the axe, I've got to cut down the beanstalk.
NARRATOR:	He chopped as fast as he could. The giant climbed down, down, down.
JACK:	The beanstalk is starting to fall. Look out, here comes the giant.
NARRATOR:	Crash!!
JACK & MOTHER:	Well, looks like that's the end of the giant.
JACK:	And that's the end of the beanstalk, too.
NARRATOR:	Jack and his mother, the hen that lays the golden eggs, and the lovely harp lived happily ever after.

In the first part of their books, Kathy Latrobe and Mildred Laughlin include readers theatre scripts based on stories from the classics. Later they show the teacher how to work with contemporary literature to develop powerful scenes for readers theatre (*The Disappearance* by Rosa Guy is a good example). In their book *Readers Theatre for Children*, Laughlin and Latrobe suggest (1) activities to prepare children to participate in readers theatre, (2) completed scripts of classics that can be introduced to children, and (3) suggested scenes from contemporary children's literature, which children may use to develop their own scripts. The *Charlotte's Web* script (on page 78) is from this third section.

THE DISAPPEARANCE*
Rosa Guy

This suggested scene is taken from chapter 12 where the Aimsleys and Dora Lee are alone in the kitchen after the police have taken Imamu away.

SUGGESTED STAGING:
The narrator stands at a lectern. Peter, Ann, Gail Aimsley, and Dora Lee sit on stools.

```
                              Peter        Ann
                                X           X

               Gail                              Dora Lee
                X                                    X

     Narrator
        X
```

NARRATOR'S OPENING LINES:
The scene that we are sharing is from *The Disappearance* by Rosa Guy. Three of the characters in this scene are from the Aimsley family. Gail Aimsley is a sensitive young adult, read by _____; Peter Aimsley is Gail's father, read by _____; and Ann Aimsley is Gail's mother, read by _____. Dora Lee is an old family friend, read by _____. I, _____, am the narrator.

This scene occurs at a crisis point for the Aimsley family. Perk, the adored younger daughter, is missing. The police have just left, taking with them the main character, Imamu Jones, as a suspect. A major clue implicating Imamu is the assumption that blood found near the sink is that of Perk, the missing child. However, the blood stains are Imamu's, and they were left there after he accidentally broke one of Ann Aimsley's crystal glasses. The mother, Ann, feels that Imamu is guilty and blames herself because she brought Imamu into their middle-class household to give him an opportunity to succeed away from dirty Harlem streets.

SCRIPTING NOTES:
1. Begin the scene with Ann Aimsley's sobbing that the disappearance is her fault.

2. Each reader will need clear instructions about the emotions that are portrayed. Dora Lee is confused; Ann is self-pitying; Peter is confused and yet desperately trying to console his wife; Gail is embarrassed and angry. Instruct each reader separately before the first lines are read.

3. Continue to convey the emotion of the scene by providing instructions for each reader. Adapt clues from the text (e.g., shouted, whimpering, and screamed).

4. In order to communicate the action of Gail in search of the broken glass and counting the pieces of crystal, create appropriate lines to be read by the narrator.

5. End the scene with Dora Lee's offer that Imamu can stay with her. Instruct the Aimsleys to stare at her.

NARRATOR'S CLOSING LINES:
Betrayed by a hysterical family that only the day before had offered friendship, Imamu Jones must find the strength within himself not only to prove his innocence but also to find the missing child.

*Reprinted with permission of Libraries Unlimited, from *Readers Theatre for Young Adults*, Englewood, Colo., 1989.

CHARLOTTE'S WEB*
E. B. White

This suggested script is from chapter 7, "Bad News," in which Wilbur learns why he is being fattened up.

SUGGESTED STAGING:
The narrator stands at a lectern. Charlotte, Wilbur, Fern, and the old sheep sit on stools.

	Wilbur	Fern	
	X	X	
Charlotte			The old sheep
X			X
Narrator			
X			

NARRATOR'S OPENING LINES:
The scene we are sharing is from *Charlotte's Web* by E. B. White. The characters in this scene are Charlotte, a spider and Wilbur's loyal friend, read by _____; Wilbur, a young and immature pig, read by _____; Fern, a little girl who is Wilbur's caretaker, read by _____; and the old sheep, read by _____. I, _____, am the narrator.

Wilbur has grown larger and fatter since Fern sold him to Mr. Zuckerman. He enjoys spending long hours sleeping and dreaming in Zuckerman's barn. On this particular afternoon Fern, Charlotte, and the old sheep are visiting with him.

SUGGESTIONS FOR SCRIPTING:
1. Begin the scene with the old sheep's comment that Wilbur is putting on weight.

2. Although Fern does not have a speaking part, she should hold a script, and she should be given instructions to react to the bad news. For example, when Wilbur first screams, Fern sits rigidly on her stool.

3. Wilbur screams and cries with fear, and the reader should be given instructions to interpret his lines with great emotion.

4. Charlotte is brisk and confident, and her reader should be given clues for interpreting her lines.

5. The old sheep is gruff, and at the end of the scene she is snapping at Wilbur. Those clues for interpreting her personality should be given to her reader.

6. End the scene with Charlotte's comment that she cannot stand hysterics.

NARRATOR'S CLOSING LINES:
Wilbur likes Charlotte. He appreciates her sensible and useful campaign against flies. However, in the months to come Charlotte will grow into a warm and true friend even more resourceful than those in the barn can imagine.

---

*Reprinted with permission of Libraries Unlimited, from *Readers Theatre for Children*, Englewood, Colo., 1990.

BIBLIOGRAPHY

Coger, L. I., and Melvin White. *Readers Theatre Handbook*. Rev. ed. Glenview, Ill: Scott, Foresman, 1973.

Fleischman, Paul. *I Am Phoenix*. New York: Harper and Row, 1985.

_____. *Joyful Mouse*. New York: Harper and Row, 1988.

Latrobe, Kathy Howard, and Mildred Knight Laughlin. *Readers Theatre for Young Adults*. Englewood, Colo.: Teacher Ideas Press, 1989.

Laughlin, Mildred Knight, and Kathy Howard Latrobe. *Readers Theatre for Children*. Englewood, Colo.: Teacher Ideas Press, 1990.

5 Pictures to Tell or Write About

Pictures can serve as an excellent stimuli for creative storytelling. Pictures are everywhere—in magazines, photo albums, newspapers, books, art museums, children's art work, and on posters and postcards. Children should find a picture and create a story to tell to a small group.

This chapter offers several "stories from pictures" ideas. These activities can serve as models for students' original work. Three artist-drawn pictures are included, with word banks already developed. Both the picture and the words should be a stimulus for story creation. The reader will find eight intriguing photographs that should also serve as a source for story development. Sometimes all students need are picture ideas or wordless picture books to stimulate their imagination. Both picture ideas and a bibliography of wordless books are included in the chapter.

►ACTIVITIES

STORIES FROM PICTURES WITH WORD BANKS

Pictures with word banks follow. Have children select a picture, review the idea word bank, and create an original story for telling.

(Text continues on page 84.)

IDEA WORDS				
storytelling	bed	flopped	bear	life
happy	jump	animals	giraffe	spring
stuffed toys	dance	dog	excited	mattress
awake	performance	stage	actors	

IDEA WORDS

door	relative	welcoming	parent	delivery person
knock	visitor	principal	introduce	surprise
open	police officer	teacher	step in	van
strange	repair person	visiting	entering	mystery
friend				

IDEA WORDS

surprise	pet	peer	game	believe	treasure
box	mystery	hole	here	inside	explore
empty	beckoning	earth	point	birthday	observe
loading	discovered	adventure	explaining	bottom	

► **ACTIVITY**

STORIES FROM PHOTOGRAPHS

Both realistic and abstract photographs can serve as stimuli for storytelling. Wayne Gundmundson and Mark Vinz were artists-in-residence in the Fargo, North Dakota, public schools. In their residency they emphasized the connection between the photographic image and the written one. Using Gundmundson's inspiring photographs as the basis, Vinz worked with the children in poetry writing. Gundmundson has permitted us to use some of his pictures in this book.

The teacher may wish to duplicate Gundmundson's pictures so that each child has a copy. Students will brainstorm ideas for their own word bank before they begin their stories. The bibliography at the end of the chapter contains several photography books, including several by Wayne Gundmundson.

Other photography books may be used as story stimuli. The photographs in any of these books could be used for creative storytelling.

PHOTOGRAPHED BY GUNDMUNDSON

(Text continues on page 92.)

PHOTOGRAPHED BY GUNDMUNDSON

PHOTOGRAPHED BY GUNDMUNDSON

PHOTOGRAPHED BY GUNDMUNDSON

PHOTOGRAPHED BY GUNDMUNDSON

PHOTOGRAPHED BY GUNDMUNDSON

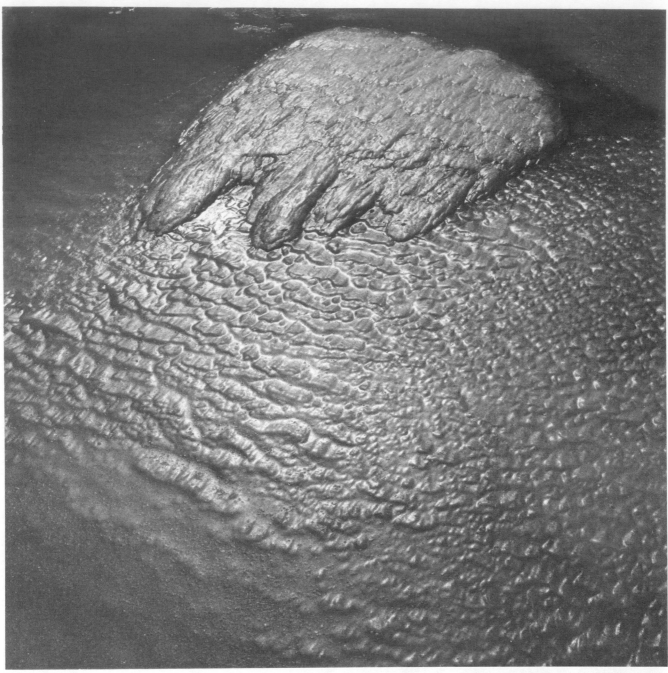

PHOTOGRAPHED BY GUNDMUNDSON

PHOTOGRAPHED BY GUNDMUNDSON

►ACTIVITIES

DRAW AND TELL

The storytellers will draw their own pictures and then make up a story to tell to the class. Students may use the form in figure 5.1 to create a story.

DRAW AND TELL STORIES ABOUT PICTURES

Look at a work of art. Make a sketch of it in the box above.

Who or what is the picture about? _____

What complication could occur in the picture to write or tell a story about? _____

_____

Where does this picture take place? _____

_____

When does this scene take place? _____

_____

NOTES FOR CREATING A STORY ABOUT A PICTURE

What happens at the beginning of the story? _____

_____

What happens at the end of the story? _____

_____

Fig. 5.1.

►ACTIVITIES

PICTURES TO DRAW AND WRITE ABOUT

Students may wish to draw pictures based on one of the suggestions below, then create stories to go with their pictures.

- A strange creature
- The frog who lost its croak
- The dinosaurs are back!
- Something's in the box!
- When everything went wrong
- Someone saying, "It's Magic!"
- A strange costume party
- Something in a child's desk talking to him or her
- Children inside a hideout, clubhouse, or tree house
- Aunt Alta's attic
- The enormous bubble (blown from a hula hoop?)
- Elves busy at work
- "I'm soaked!"
- A shadow that comes alive
- A box that has "My New Invention" printed on it
- If snow were all colors!
- The practical joke!
- It was like magic!
- Some day I want to go ...

WORDLESS BOOKS

Younger children in particular would enjoy "reading" a wordless book and then telling their version of the story. A bibliography of wordless books is included at the end of the chapter.

YOU'RE ON YOUR OWN

Students can go on a picture hunt and find their own pictures to tell about.

BIBLIOGRAPHY

Wordless Books

Alexander, Martha. *Bobo's Dream*. New York: Dial, 1970.

Amoss, Berthe. *What Did You Lose, Santa?* New York: Harper and Row, 1987.

Anno, Mitsumasa. *Anno's Britain*. New York: Philomel, 1982.

_____. *Anno's Counting Book*. New York: Harper and Row, 1977.

_____. *Anno's Flea Market*. New York: Philomel, 1984.

Bang, Molly. *The Grey Lady and the Strawberry Snatcher*. New York: Four Winds, 1980.

Briggs, Raymond. *Building the Snowman*. Boston: Little, Brown, 1985.

_____. *The Snowman*. New York: Random House, 1978.

Carle, Eric. *Do You Want to Be My Friend?* New York: Crowell, 1971.

Collington, Peter. *The Angel and the Soldier Boy*. New York: Knopf/Borzoi, 1987.

deGroat, Diane. *Alligator's Toothache*. New York: Crown, 1977.

dePaola, Tomie. *Flicks*. New York: Harcourt Brace Jovanovich, 1979.

_____. *Sing, Pierrot, Sing: A Picture Book of Mime*. New York: Harcourt Brace Jovanovich, 1983.

Drescher, Henrik. *The Yellow Umbrella*. New York: Bradbury, 1987.

Dupasquier, Philippe. *The Great Escape*. New York: Houghton Mifflin, 1988.

Florian, Douglas. *Airplane Ride*. New York: Crowell, 1984.

Goodall, John. *Creepy Castle*. New York: Atheneum, 1975.

_____. *Naughty Nancy Goes to School*. New York: McElderry, 1985.

_____. *Paddy to the Rescue*. New York: McElderry, 1985.

_____. *Paddy's Evening Out*. New York: McElderry, 1973.

Hoban, Tana. *Is It Red? Is It Yellow? Is It Blue?* New York: Greenwillow, 1978.

_____. *Look! Look! Look!* New York: Greenwillow, 1988.

Hutchins, Pat. *Changes, Changes*. New York: Macmillan, 1971.

Keats, Ezra Jack. *Pssst! Doggie*. New York: Franklin Watts, 1973.

Kitchen, Bert. *Animal Alphabet*. New York: Dial, 1984.

Krahn, Fernando. *The Mystery of the Giant Footprints*. New York: Dutton, 1977.

_____. *Robot-Bot-Bot*. New York: Dutton, 1979.

Mayer, Mercer. *A Boy, a Dog and a Frog*. New York: Dial, 1967.

_____. *Bubble, Bubble*. New York: Parents, 1973.

_____. *Frog Goes to Dinner*. New York: Dial, 1974.

McCully, Emily. *The Christmas Gift*. New York: Harper and Row, 1985.

_____. *First Snow*. New York: Harper and Row, 1985.

_____. *New Baby*. New York: Harper and Row, 1988.

_____. *Picnic*. New York: Harper and Row, 1984.

_____. *School*. New York: Harper and Row, 1987.

Munro, Roxie. *Christmastime in New York City*. New York: Dodd, Mead, 1987.

Ormerod, Jan. *Moonlight*. New York: Lothrop, Lee and Shepard, 1982.

Prater, John. *The Gift*. New York: Viking-Penguin/Puffin Books, 1986.

Saltzberg, Barney. *The Yawn*. New York: Atheneum, 1985.

Spier, Peter. *Peter Spier's Rain*. New York: Doubleday, 1981.

Tafuri, Nancy. *Have You Seen My Duckling?* New York: Greenwillow, 1985.

Turkle, Brinton. *Deep in the Forest*. New York: Dutton, 1976.

Ungerer, Tomi. *Snail, Where Are You?* New York: Harper and Row, 1962.

Ward, Lynd. *The Silver Pony*. New York: Houghton Mifflin, 1973.

Wiesner, David. *Free Fall*. New York: Lothrop, Lee and Shepard, 1988.

Winter, Paula. *The Bear and the Fly*. New York: Crown, 1987.

Young, Ed. *The Other Bone*. New York: Harper and Row, 1984.

Photographs

Blumenfeld, Milton. *Careers in Photography*. Minneapolis: Lerner, 1979.

Freedman, Russel. *Lincoln (A Photobiography)*. New York: Clarion, 1987.

Freeman, Tony. *A New True Book, Photography*. Prepared under the direction of Illa Podendorf. Chicago: Children's Press, 1983.

Gundmundson, Wayne. *Iron Spirit*. Fargo: North Dakota Council on the Arts, 1982.

_____. *A Long Way to See*. Fargo: North Dakota State University, Institute for Regional Studies, 1987.

Meltzer, Milton. *Dorothea Lange: Life through the Camera (Women of Our Time)*. Illustrations by Donna Diamond and photographs by Dorothea Lange. New York: Viking-Kestrel, 1985.

Photographs from the Williston Basin. Moorhead, Minn.: Acme Invisible, Inc., 1982.

Surfrin, Mark. *Focus on America (Profiles of Nine Photographers)*. New York: Scribner, 1987.

Frames for Pictures and Stories

Kinghorn, Harriet. *V.I.P. Frames: Animals*. Illustrated by Richard Wells. Forest Lake, Minn.: Teacher Touch, 1987. (Reproducible books)

_____. *V.I.P. Frames: Holidays*. Illustrated by Richard Wells. Forest Lake, Minn.: Teacher Touch, 1987. (Reproducible books)

6 Storytelling Totes

Children of all ages will enjoy creating storytelling totes, designed by Harriet Kinghorn and Richard Wells and then telling stories using their creations. Young children can make them for themselves, whereas older students can create them for, or with, younger children. The process is simple.

Children may select an animal from the patterns printed on pages 100-118, or they may create their own characters, animals, or objects. They then color or decorate the patterns, cut them out, and glue them onto their bags. Notice that most of the animal patterns have a front and a back.

The teacher may wish to have the children read several books about an animal before they begin writing and telling original stories. Suggestions are provided in the bibliography at the end of the chapter. Students then write or record stories making simple paper props that go with the stories. As they tell their stories, they put the props into their bags. Students may prefer to use real objects as Pelton did in her story "Not Carrots." After telling their stories at school, the children can take their storytelling totes home and tell the stories to their families.

Children may want to experiment with original creations. For example, they might turn their totes into big black pots and tell the story "Stone Soup." They could put all the ingredients for stone soup into their "pots" as the story unfolds. Two examples of storytelling with totes follow. The first is called "Too Many Feet."

Materials: Paper tote bags, patterns of caterpillar and shoes, crayons or markers, glue, scissors, construction paper, and the story.

Directions: Students cut out the caterpillar (page 100) and the shoes (pages 101-2), color them, and attach the caterpillar to their bags. The students lay the shoes out in front of them in the order in which they appear in the story. The students tell the story, putting the shoes into the bag each time they are rejected by the caterpillar.

Too Many Feet
Mary Helen Pelton

Harold is a caterpillar. As an elongated wormlike creature he has special problems. For example, can you imagine trying to get through a revolving door without getting squashed when you are that long and skinny. If you're a caterpillar you have to be especially careful crossing the street. Your front half has to keep moving even after it's safely across the street, or your back end could look like it's been run over by the Incredible Hulk.

Harold makes it safely across the street and into the department store, excited about buying new shoes. He has to buy eight pairs to be exact, because that's how many pairs of feet he has. First he tries on these [hold up old-fashioned shoes].

"No!" says Harold. "Those aren't for me" [put shoes into tote].

Next he tries on these [sandals].

"No! I don't think so," says Harold. "They look like something out of the sixties—not at all for me" [shoes into tote].

"Hey, these aren't bad [engineering boots]. No, they would be too heavy with eight pairs on my feet; they would weigh more than I do" [shoes into tote].

Next he tries on these [ballet slippers—into tote].

"No, I don't dance."

The shoe salesman says, "Well, how about these?" [ice-skates]

No, caterpillars can't coordinate their feet well enough to play hockey," explains Harold [skates into tote].

Next the shoe salesman offers, "Hmm—maybe these" [flippers].

"No! Great for frogs but not for caterpillars. I kind of like these [running shoes]. Nice, but the last time I tried to run I stepped on my own feet and ended up in a terrible tangle" [shoes into tote].

"Hmm, what about these" [high-top tennis shoes], the shoe salesman suggests.

My goodness, by the time I got up in the morning and got those all laced up, it would be time to go to bed," says Harold.

"These are just the thing," says the shoe salesman [loafers].

"Those are perfect! Wonderful, terrific!! I love 'em, I'll take eight pairs," exclaims Harold.

But the shoe salesman says, "I'm sorry but we only have two pairs left."

"Well, how about these?" [very colorful]

"No!"

"These?" [very ugly]

"No!"

"These?" [funny-looking]

"No!"

Just then Harold sees another caterpillar walking by in the store, barefooted and wearing a beautiful sweater. "Excuse me!" says Harold. "Would you please direct me to the sweater department. Maybe caterpillars should go around barefoot after all."

The second example of storytelling with totes is called "Not Carrots."

Materials: Paper bag, pattern of rabbit (page 103), crayons or markers, glue, scissors, construction paper, carrots, chocolate bar, peanut butter and jelly sandwich, acorns, worm, grass, fish, bone, and corn cobs. (If the real objects are not available, students can draw pictures of the food that goes inside the tote.)

Directions: Students cut out the rabbit, color it and attach it to the tote. Students collect the objects that go into the tote. The students lay the objects out in the order in which they appear in the story. The students tell the story putting the objects into the bag each time they are suggested by a character.

Alternate Directions: Students cut out the rabbit, color it and attach it to the tote. Each student creates a story about the rabbit and makes a list of objects needed to tell the story. After objects have been collected or pictures drawn of the objects, students are ready to begin.

Not Carrots
Mary Helen Pelton

"Carrots—I love them," said Becky Bunny. "What could be better than a cold, crisp carrot!" [hold carrot up, then put it aside]

A little boy overheard Becky and said, "Oh, peanut butter and jelly sandwiches are much better than carrots. You should try them" [peanut butter and jelly sandwich into tote]. So Becky ate it, but it stuck to the roof of her mouth, and the jelly squirted out all over her pretty white coat.

"Try this," said a little girl who was walking by eating a chocolate bar [chocolate bar into tote]. It looked good, so Becky ate it, but the chocolate melted all over her paws and made them sticky and brown.

"No, no, no," said the squirrel, "acorns are the best." So Becky tried to eat four but couldn't even break the shell, so she had to swallow them whole (gulp!) [acorns into tote].

"Worms," said the robin, bringing Becky a great big, juicy, wiggly, slimy worm. Becky ate it, [worm into tote] but it wiggled and turned and jiggled and jiggled all the way down. "Very icky," thought Becky.

The cow was horrified! "No, no, no! Not worms or acorns—grass. Green, crunchy grass—hummmmmm." Becky grabbed a handful [grass into tote]. "Not bad," said Becky, "but not carrots either."

A cat brought her a fish [fish into tote]. The dog, a bone [bone into tote]. The pig, corn cobs [cobs into tote]. But Becky was so full she felt sick. "Right now I couldn't eat a thing. But carrots still are the best." She shared carrots with all of her friends. They crunched and munched on those crispy, cool carrots.

"Not bad," they said, "but peanut butter sandwiches, chocolate bars, acorns, worms, grass, fish, bones, and corn cobs are still the best."

"Well, to each his own," thought Becky Bunny [put carrots into tote]. Then she hopped off and decided that maybe she would just keep the carrots for herself.

Additional patterns for a variety of creatures and animals are included at the end of the chapter, as well as a bibliography of both fiction and nonfiction stories about each animal. Have students read the stories and then create original tales or retell one of the stories, using the storytelling totes. As students read, they may wish to take notes on the storytelling tote form in figure 6.1 to remind them of information they would like to include in their stories. They can then create original tales (and original totes) or retell a story from a book about their storytelling tote character. Students will particularly enjoy making creative props to include with their story.

(Text continues on page 119.)

STORY REPORT
(for Storytelling Totes)

Creature _____   Reporter _____

_____
(Title of the book I read)

_____
(Author of the book)

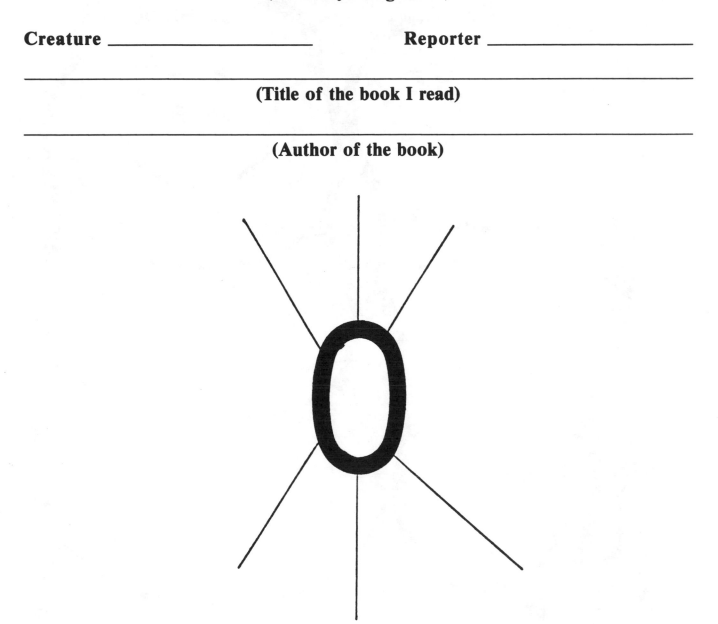

Fig. 6.1.

Caterpillar pattern

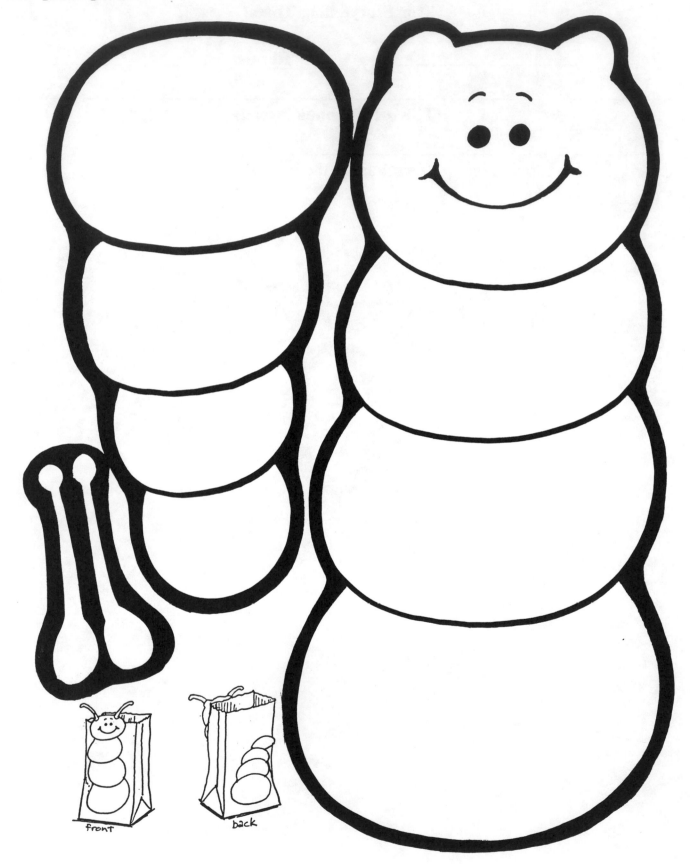

Shoe patterns

Bunny pattern

Ears could be flopped near the top.

Glue ears behind head.

Glue

Glue

Cut on heavy black lines.

Cut in

Cut into dotted lines

Glue

Fold at dotted lines

back

Glue   Tail

Front

This tail could be replaced with a wad of cotton.

Turkey pattern

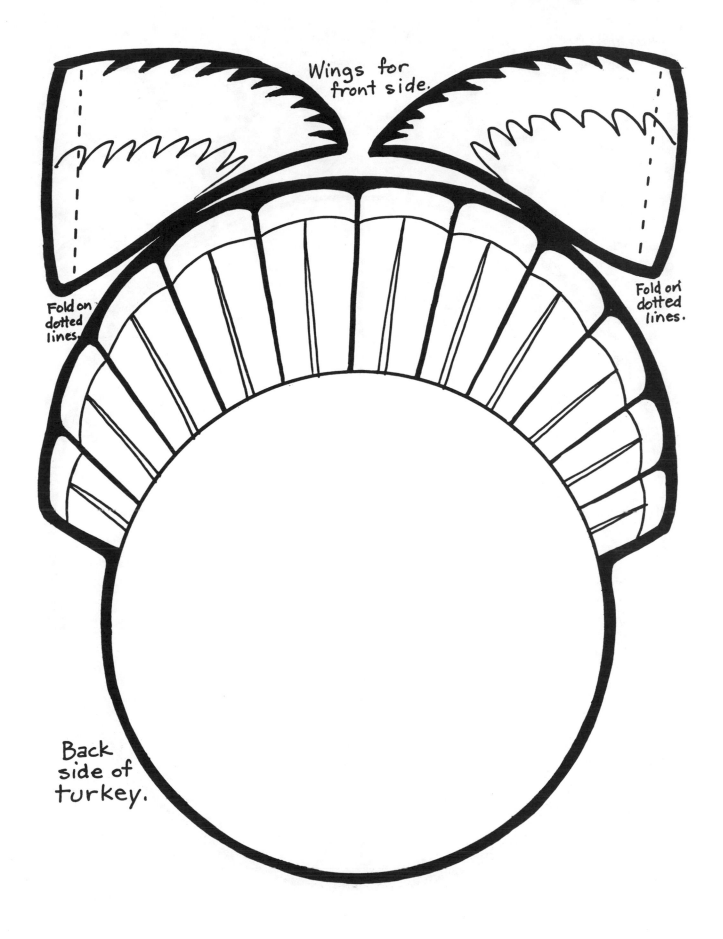

Wings for front side.

Fold on dotted lines.

Fold on dotted lines.

Back side of turkey.

Ladybug pattern

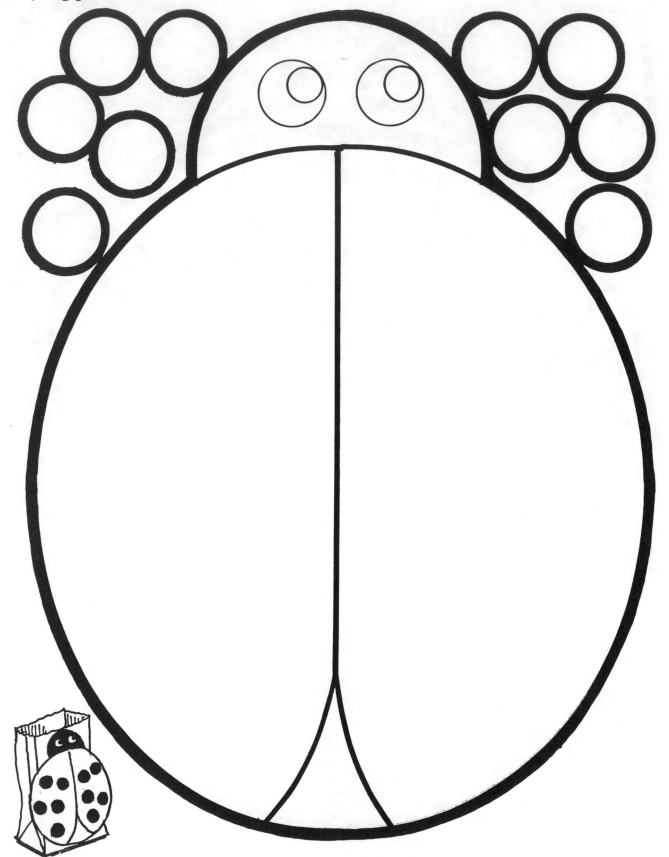

Frog pattern

Turtle pattern

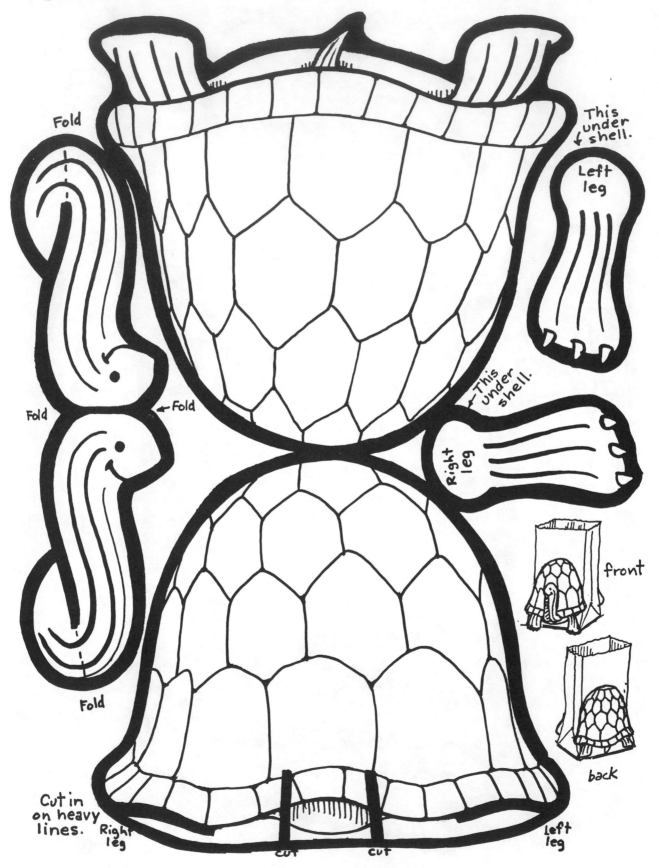

Fold

This under shell.

Left leg

Fold

Fold

This under shell.

Right leg

front

back

Cut in on heavy lines.

Right leg

cut

cut

Left leg

Cow pattern

Bend ears forward.

Horns

Glue

Glue

tail

back

front

Dog pattern

Paw

Fold on
dotted lines

Glue

Paw

Ear

Ear

back

front

Horse pattern

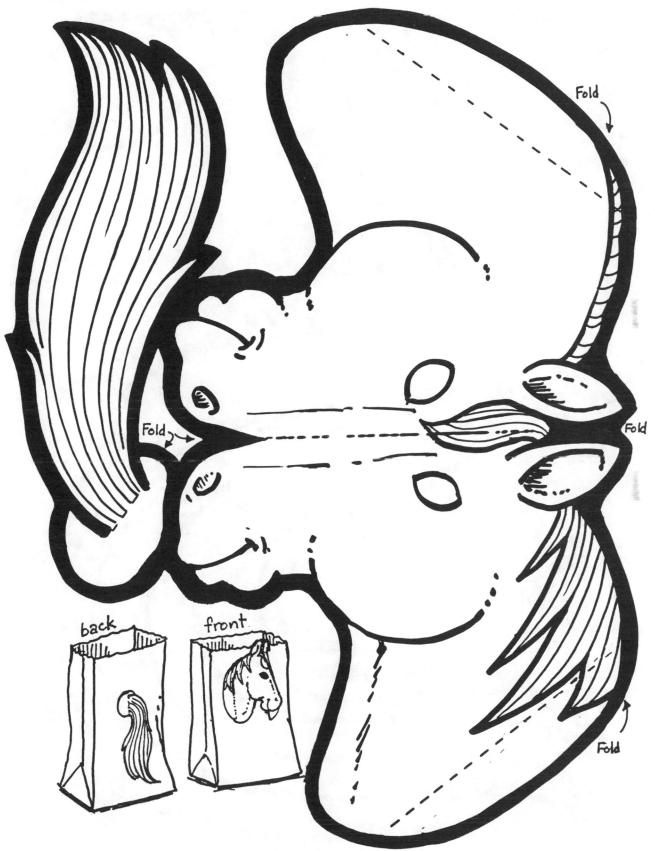

back   front

Fold

Fold

Fold

Fold

Rooster pattern

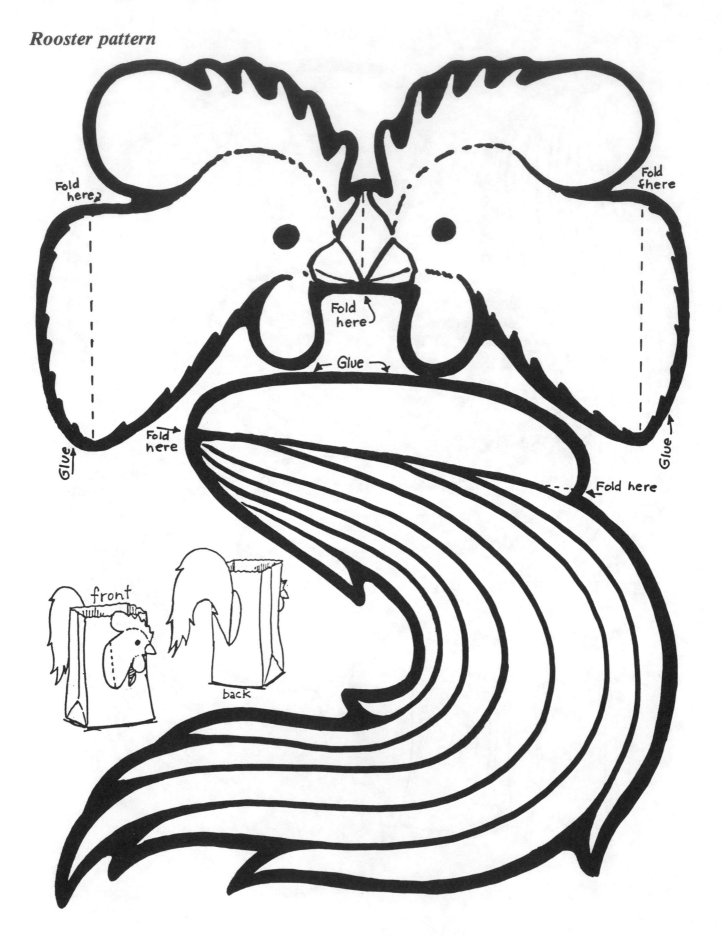

Goat pattern

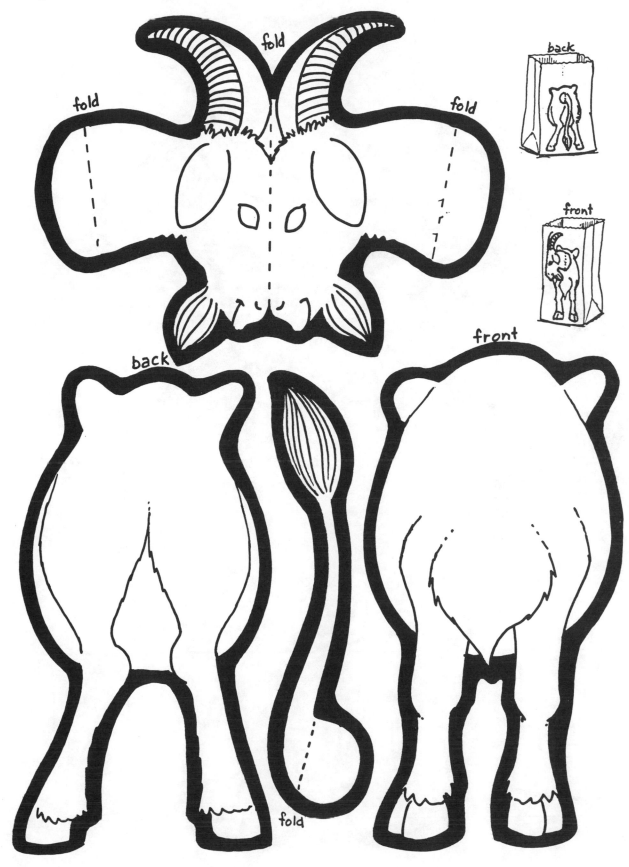

Sheep pattern

Glue

Cut all heavy black lines.

Cut down for neck and crease on dotted lines.

back

front

Cat pattern

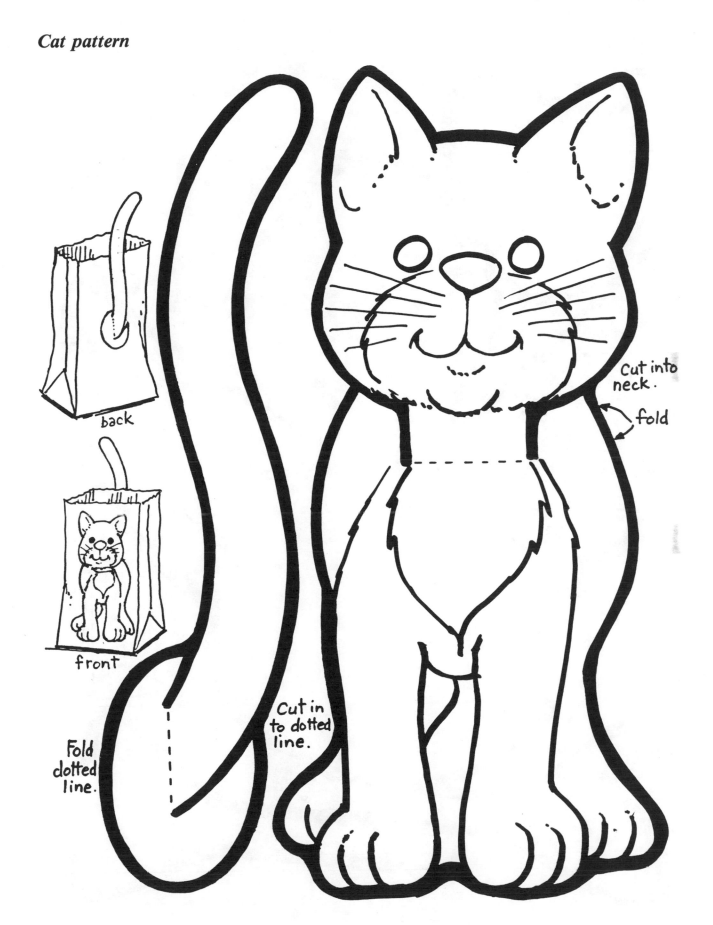

back

front

Cut into neck.

fold

Cut in to dotted line.

Fold dotted line.

Duck pattern

Pig pattern

Ears

Glue

Glue

Tail

Glue

Glue

Fold ears like this.

Cut out tail so it can spring out, crease in spots so it sticks out.

back

front

Hen and chicks pattern

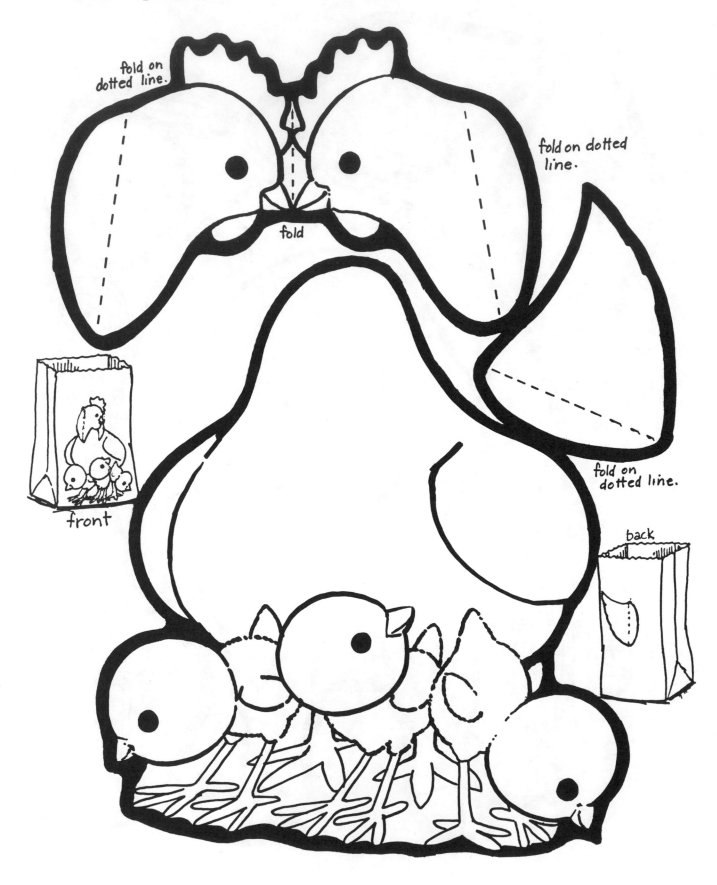

fold on dotted line.

fold on dotted line.

fold

fold on dotted line.

front

back

BIBLIOGRAPHY

Cat

Gag, Wanda. *Millions of Cats*. New York: Coward, McCann, 1928; 1977. (Fiction)

Jameson, J. *Cats (Responsible Pet Care Series)*. Vero Beach, Fla.: Rourke, 1990. (Nonfiction)

Matthias, Catherine. *I Love Cats*. Illustrated by Tom Dunnington. Chicago: Children's Press, 1983. (Fiction)

Selsam, Millicent E., and Hoyce Hunt. *A First Look at Cats*. Illustrated by Harriett Springer. New York: Walker, 1981. (Nonfiction)

Caterpillar

Carle, Eric. *The Very Hungry Caterpillar*. New York: Philomel, 1969; Putnam, 1986. (Fiction)

Kent, Jack. *The Caterpillar and the Polliwog*. Englewood Cliffs, N.J.: Prentice Hall, 1986. (Fiction)

O'Hagan, Caroline (advisory ed.). *It's Easy to Have a Caterpillar Visit You*. Illustrated by Judith Allan. New York: Lothrop, Lee and Shepard, 1980. (Fiction)

Reidel, Marlene. *From Egg to Butterfly*. Minneapolis: Carolrhoda, 1981. (Nonfiction)

Cow

Gibbons, Gail. *The Milk Makers*. New York: Macmillan, 1985. (Nonfiction)

Jewell, Nancy. *Calf, Goodnight*. Illustrated by Leonard Weisgard. New York: Harper and Row, 1973. (Fiction)

Krasilovsky, Phyllis. *The Cow Who Fell in the Canal*. Illustrated by Peter Spier. New York: Doubleday, 1957. (Fiction)

Moon, Cliff. *Dairy Cows on the Farm*. Illustrated by Anna Jupp. New York: Bookwright, 1983. (Nonfiction)

Dog

Cole, Joanna. *A Dog's Body*. Photographs by Jam and Ann Monteith. New York: William Morris, 1986. (Nonfiction)

Gackenbach, Dick. *A Bag Full of Pups*. New York: Clarion, 1981.

Jameson, P. *Dogs (Responsible Pet Care Series)*. Vero Beach, Fla.: Rourke, 1990. (Nonfiction)

Lipkind, William, and Nicolas Mordvinoff. *Finders Keepers*. New York: Harcourt, Brace and World, 1951. (Fiction)

Duck

Daimals, Anne-Marie. *The Duck (Animal World)*. Illustrated by Peter Barrett. Windermere, Fla.: Rourke, 1983. (Nonfiction)

Dunn, Judy. *The Little Duck*. Illustrated by Phoebe Dunn. New York: Random House, 1976. (Nonfiction)

McCloskey, Robert. *Make Way for Ducklings*. New York: Viking, 1941; New York: Puffin, 1976. (Fiction)

Miles, Miska. *Swim, Little Duck*. Illustrated by Jim Arnosky. Boston: Little, Brown, 1976. (Fiction)

Frog

Dallinger, Jane, and Sylvia A. Johnson. *The World of Frogs and Toads*. Photographs by Hiroshi Tanemura. Minneapolis: Lerner, 1982. (Nonfiction)

Florian, Douglas. *Discovering Frogs*. New York: Scribner, 1988. (Nonfiction)

Lobel, Arnold. *Frog and Toad Together*. New York: Harper, 1972. (Fiction)

West, Colin. *"Hello, Great Big Bullfrog!"* New York: Lippincott, 1987. (Fiction)

Goat

Chiefari, Janet. *Kids Are Baby Goats*. New York: Dodd, Mead, 1984. (Nonfiction)

Lavine, Sigmund A., and Vincent Scuro. *Wonders of Goats*. New York: Dodd, Mead, 1980. (Nonfiction)

Pizer, Abigail. *Hattie the Goat*. Minneapolis: Carolrhoda, 1989.

Hen and Chick

Back, Christine, and Jens Olesen. *Chicken and Egg*. Photographs by Bo Jarner. Morristown, N.J.: Silver Burdett, 1986. (Nonfiction)

Ginsburg, Mirra. *Good Morning, Chick*. Illustrated by Byron Barton. New York: Greenwillow, 1980. (Fiction)

Heller, Ruch. *Chickens Aren't the Only Ones*. New York: Grosset and Dunlap, 1981. (Nonfiction)

Oakley, Graham. *Hetty and Harriet*. New York: Atheneum, 1981. (Fiction)

Horse

Goble, Paul. *The Girl Who Loved Wild Horses*. New York: Bradbury, 1978. (Fiction)

Locker, Thomas. *The Mare on the Hill*. New York: Dial, 1985. (Fiction)

Lundell, Margo. *Harold Roth's Big Book of Horses*. Photographs by Harold Roth. New York: Grosset, 1987. (Nonfiction)

Selsam, Millicent E., and Joyce Hunt. *A First Look at Horses*. Illustrated by Harriet Springer. New York: Walker, 1981.

Ladybug

Brown, Ruth. *Ladybug, Ladybug*. New York: Dutton, 1988. (Fiction)

Carle, Eric. *The Grouchy Ladybug*. New York: Harper and Row, 1977. (Fiction)

Pouyanne, Therese. *The Ladybug (Animal World)*. Illustrated by Masako Shimada. Windermere, Fla.: Rourke, 1983. (Nonfiction)

Watts, Barrie. *Ladybug*. Jamestown, N.J.: Silver Burdett, 1987. (Nonfiction)

Pig

Christelow, Eileen. *Mr. Murphy's Marvelous Invention*. New York: Houghton Mifflin, 1983. (Fiction)

Dunn, Judy. *The Little Pig*. Photographs by Phoebe Dunn. New York: Random House, 1987. (Nonfiction)

Hinds, Mignon P. *Baby Pigs*. Illustrated by Jim Kritz. Stamford, Conn.: Longmeadow, 1988. (Nonfiction)

Lamont, Priscilla. *The Troublesome Pig*. New York: Crown, 1983. (Fiction)

Rabbit

Dunn, Judy. *The Little Rabbit*. Photographs by Phoebe Dunn. New York: Random House, 1978. (Nonfiction)

Heyward, Du Bose. *The Country Bunny and the Little Gold Shoes*. Illustrated by Marjorie Flack. Boston: Houghton Mifflin, 1976. (Fiction)

Potter, Beatrix. *Peter Rabbit*. New York: Warne, 1986. (Fiction)

Rooster

Chaucer, Geoffrey, and Barbara Cooney. *Chanticleer and the Fox*. Adapted and Illustrated by Barbara Cooney. New York: Crowell, 1958. (Fiction)

Mathews, Louise. *Cluck One*. Illustrated by Jeni Bassett. New York: Dodd, Mead, 1982. (Fiction)

Sheep

Ernst, Lisa Campbell. *Nattie Parsons' Good-Luck Lamb*. New York: Viking-Kestrel, 1988. (Fiction)

Mitgutsch, Ali. *From Sheep to Scarf*. Minneapolis: Carolrhoda, 1971. (Nonfiction)

Panek, Dennis. *Ba Ba Sheep Wouldn't Go to Sleep*. New York: Franklin Watts, 1988. (Fiction)

Spanjian, Beth. *Baby Lamb*. Illustrated by John Butler. Stamford, Conn.: Longmeadow, 1988. (Nonfiction)

Turkey

Barth, Edna. *Turkeys, Pilgrims and Indian Corn: The Story of the Thanksgiving Symbols*. Illustrations by Ursula Arndt. New York: Clarion, 1975. (Nonfiction)

Miller, Edna. *Mousekin's Thanksgiving*. Englewood Cliffs, N.J.: Prentice Hall, 1985. (Fiction)

Patent, Dorothy Hinshaw. *Wild Turkey, Tame Turkey*. Photographs by William Munoz. New York: Clarion, 1990. (Nonfiction)

Quackenbush, Robert. *Sheriff Sally Gopher and the Thanksgiving Caper*. New York: Lothrop, Lee and Shepard, 1982. (Fiction)

Turtle

Craig, Janet. *Turtles (Now I Know)*. Illustrated by Kathie Kelleher. Mahwah, N.J.: Troll Associates, 1982. (Nonfiction)

Metral, Yvette. *The Turtle (Animal World)*. Illustrated by Charlotte Knox. Mahwah, N.J.: Troll Associates, 1983. (Nonfiction)

Seuss, Dr. *Yertle the Turtle and Other Stories*. New York: Random House, 1958. (Fiction)

Thaler, Mike. *In the Middle of the Puddle*. Illustrated by Bruce Degen. New York: Harper and Row, 1988. (Fiction)

Creating Stories with Plate-Oramas

Students may develop creative Plate-Oramas with original stories for telling both at home and at school. The Plate-Oramas, designed by Harriet Kinghorn, can serve as centerpieces and as props for storytelling.

Materials: Paper plate, glue, colored paper, crayons or markers, string, paper clips, scissors, patterns (in this chapter)

Directions: The students select one of the following stories to use as a starter for their Plate-Orama. The students cut out and color appropriate characters and props and glue them to the plate. Students may create their own characters or the teacher can reproduce the patterns on pages 128-129 for them. The scenes for the Plate-Oramas can be designed similar to the ones in the illustrations or the students can plan and create their own.

The stories in this section can be reproduced for each student. Some children may choose to use the patterns for their first Plate-Oramas, while others will enjoy creating their own from the very beginning.

Procedure: Read this story and make a Plate-Orama. Retell the story in your own words.

I Hate Fishing

Mary Helen Pelton

My whole family loves to fish, except me, that is. Dad and Mom fix the picnic, and my big sister and brother hitch the boat to the car. When we get to the lake my brother stays on the dock. I help my dad row the boat to the center of the lake. I make faces at my brother on the dock.

My sister is a scaredy-cat. She won't put worms on the hook. "Yuk," she says.

"Wimp," I say. My mom is a semi-scaredy-cat. She wears rubber gloves when she baits her hook.

My brother has caught one perch and one sunfish by the time we get out into the middle of the lake. I should've stayed on the dock with him.

My dad catches two walleyes. My mom catches a big northern pike. My sister catches three little sunfish. I catch the bottom of the lake three times. How embarrassing!

Then my brother catches two more. My dad catches one, my mom three. I catch my sister's line and make her lose the old tennis shoe she was reeling in. I hate fishing!

We had just gotten our lines untangled and back in the water when my dad yells, "Pull in your lines. Look at the storm coming."

No sooner has he said it when the wind hits the boat. I get knocked to the bottom of the boat. Daddy works hard on the oars but it seems like a LONG time before we reach my brother on the dock. We all pull the boat out of the water.

I hadn't had time to reel in my line and it dragged in the water as daddy rowed into shore. Guess what? On the end of my line was the biggest fish of all. Maybe fishing isn't so bad after all.

Directions: If you could walk to the end of the rainbow, what treasure would you find? What would you see along the way? Read the following story as a model, then create your own Plate-Orama that shows what you'd see and what you'd find at the end of your rainbow.

The Rainbow

Mary Helen Pelton

Jason and his imaginary friend Ernie loved to play together from early morning 'til late at night. Something was different on Tuesday, however. Ernie brought another friend with him from the land of imagination.

His friend, Maria, was an elf who was only two feet tall and wore purple tights underneath her green leaf dress.

It had just stopped raining when they walked up to Jason as he sat on the front porch. "Wow, look at the rainbow," cried Jason looking over their heads.

"Did you know," said Maria, "that if you wish just right, you can find your dreams at the end of the rainbow? Why don't you wish and see what happens?"

"Oh boy, I wish for gold!" cried Ernie.

"No," said Maria, "that's not a good wish because once you have it, once you spend it, it's gone!"

"Yeah, right. OK. I wish for a super-electric-attack-man toy," said Ernie.

"What will you do when the batteries go dead?" said Maria, "Not a good wish."

"Well, I'll wish for all the cake and ice cream in the whole world to be at the end of the rainbow," suggested Jason.

"You're not getting the point," said Maria. "You couldn't eat all the ice cream and cake in the world, and if you did you'd be sick! No, not the point at all."

"Well, tell us the point then I want to get a wish," said Jason.

"Let's try it this way," said Maria, "what makes you feel really, really good and really, really happy?"

"Well," said Jason, "let's see … it makes me feel good when Dog licks my face when I get off the school bus."

"That's the right idea," said Maria.

"I feel good when my buddy Ernie is waiting for me to play each morning."

"I like to watch my baby sister play with her rattle in the crib. I feel warm and happy when I watch her."

"I felt happy when my school friend John shared his cookies with me when my mom forgot to put dessert in my lunch box."

"It really make me feel good when my mommy and daddy tell me stories before I go to bed at night."

"Yes, you got the point."

"Wish for those good things then," said Maria. "Then we'll walk all the way to the end of the rainbow and get them."

"Right," said Ernie.

"Wait a minute," said Jason, "why should I walk all the way to the end of the rainbow when I have all those things right at home?"

"Smart boy!" said Maria.

"Come on Ernie and Maria, let's forget about the rainbow and take Dog down to the pond to catch frogs. Come on I'll race you!"

As Jason, Dog, Ernie, and Maria run down to the pond, the rainbow shimmers and fades to await another day.

Directions: Everyone enjoys picnics. Students create a Plate-Orama showing their favorite kind of picnic and make up a story to share with a small group and their families.

Let's Go on a Picnic

Mary Helen Pelton

Every family has special things they take on a picnic. Before my family leaves, we try to think of *all* the important things:

> Important Things to Eat With
>
> Important Things to Eat
>
> Important Things to Play With
>
> Other Important Things

Important Things to Eat With

Mom takes out our special red and white checkered table cloth. She finds the blue plastic cups and forks and the white paper plates that blow away in the big wind. What important things to eat with would *you* take on *your* picnic?

Important Things to Eat

In our family every person gets to pick one favorite thing for the picnic. Daddy picks fried chicken. John picks potato salad. Sara picks a salad made with grapes, oranges, and pineapple. Grandma picks chocolate fudge layer cake. I pick ginger cookies. Grandpa picks the best thing of all, homemade ice cream. Mom picks coffee for the grownups and soda for the kids. (I don't really think that is her favorite thing. I think she is just being polite.) What important thing would *you* pick if you were going on our picnic?

Important Things to Play With

My dog, Jenny, and I like to play frisbee when we go on a picnic. I take my red frisbee with blue stripes. Mom and Dad like to take a net and a ball so they can play volleyball with the other grownups. My sister, Sara, doesn't have to take any equipment along because she likes to play games such as Statue and Red Rover-Red Rover with the other kids. What important things to play with would *you* take along? What games do *you* like to play when you go on a picnic?

Other Important Things

The other important things you have to take are different, depending on where you live. In Minnesota you have to take mosquito spray. In Georgia you may have to bring along red ant spray. Once we had a picnic in Florida and two big alligators crawled around near our picnic place. I wonder if there is such a thing as alligator spray. What other important things would *you* take on a picnic?

Directions: Have students go out onto the playground. Ask them: "What sounds do you hear on your playground? Let's go listen. Let's make up a song or poem or story about the sounds of the playground and create a Plate-Orama that looks like our playground. Share it with a friend."

The Playground

Mary Helen Pelton

John and Mary sit quietly on the school playground, close their eyes, and listen to the sounds they hear.

Children laughing, slides slipping, feet crunching, cars passing, birds singing, bells ringing. So different from the sounds of a living room or a classroom.

(Text continues on page 132.)

Character patterns

8 Puppets and Flannel Boards

The visual and oral worlds come together when the storyteller uses puppetry and flannel boards to tell a story. The combination is not only compelling, but delightful as well.

Children of all ages enjoy storytelling with puppets and flannel boards. However, when working with older students, the teacher must take special care when introducing the activity. The teacher might say, "We are going to work with puppets and flannel boards so that you can create something we can present to a lower-grade class. In addition, this tool will be very valuable when you babysit or work as a camp counselor."

As teachers search for appropriate stories that work well for stick puppets, three-dimensional puppets, and flannel boards, they will want to look for or create stories with the following characteristics:

- Clear simple action line

- Strong lead characters

- Minimum number of characters, props, and visual and scene changes

Although cumulative tales (those that are structured on repeated action) may have a number of characters, they still lend themselves well to puppet plays and flannel boards (for example, "Stone Soup," "Woman and the Pig," "Little Red Hen").

Puppet and flannel board characters help children to be less inhibited. Storytellers can "hide" behind characters, becoming someone or something else during the performance. Many shy children blossom when they have the opportunity to work with puppets or flannel board characters.

STICK PUPPETS

First, we will explore the use of two-dimensional characters that can be used on a simple puppet stage or on a flannel board. The puppets we will begin with are paper, designed to be colored, cut out, folded, and glued to a paper stick. The sets for the characters are designed to be worn around the neck of the puppeteer and are made from file folders (see instructions for making the puppet stage/set on p. 131). The file folder pocket is not only an excellent stage or backdrop for the puppets, but it can also be used for storing the puppets when they are not in use. Characters can be found in nursery rhymes, folktales, fairy tales, or in the imagination. Living theatre! But more than living. Stick puppets allow the theatre to move from location to location with no more disruption than a casual walk. The puppeteers move their characters back and forth across the set. Puppeteers are still free to take a part in the drama themselves. For example, in the story "Jack and the Beanstalk," the puppeteer would play the giant, towering over the little world in front of him and over small creatures in the play.

This portable, living theater has many applications and many educational advantages. The puppets and sets can be colored and laminated to be used over and over again—in learning centers, with flannel boards, and so forth. They can be duplicated by any of several processes so that all students can produce dramas not only in the classroom but also (perhaps more importantly) at home for parents and brothers and sisters. These productions call upon language skills, perceptual skills, listening skills, and organizational skills; they help to develop vocabulary, literary appreciation, and creativity.

Instructions for making puppet stage

a folded piece of
2½" tagboard forms
the bottom of the
Pocket on each side
of the File Folder.

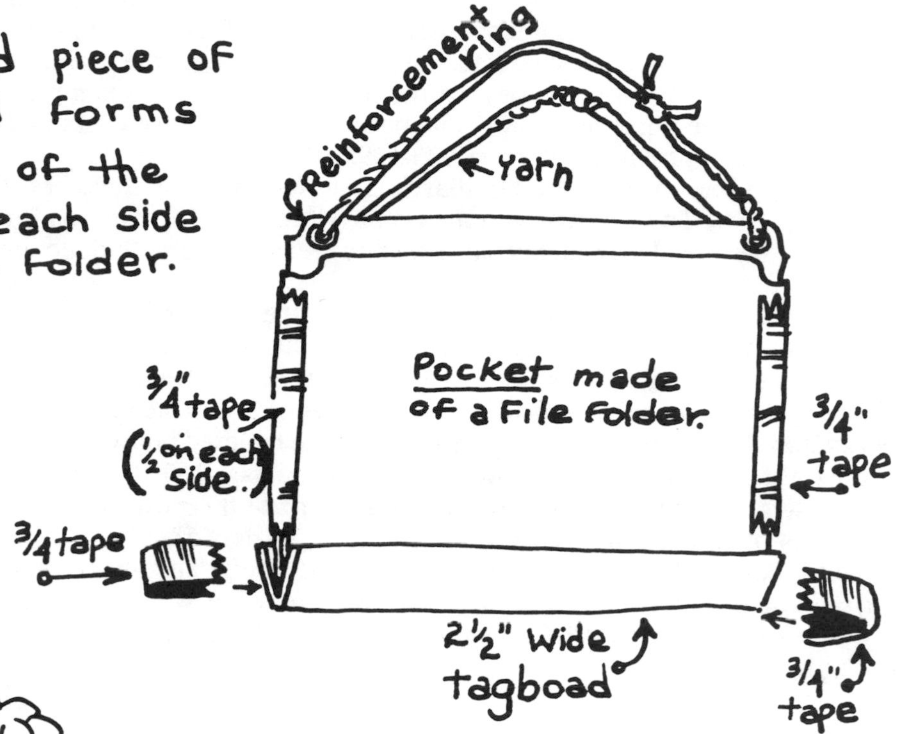

Reinforcement ring

← Yarn

Pocket made
of a File Folder.

¾" tape
(½ on each side.)

¾" tape

¾" tape →

¾" tape →

2½" wide
tagboad ↑

¾" tape ↑

Suggested uses for
the pocket.

Patterns are provided for nursery rhymes, folktales, and two original tales by Harriet Kinghorn. Students simply cut out the puppets, color them, fold them as indicated, glue them to sticks, and the characters are ready to perform. Students should also be encouraged to make their own stick puppets.

When the stage is set and the characters are poised off-stage, the drama needs only words to come to life. We suggest moving from the easiest to the most complex. For example, the puppeteer may wish to begin by retelling simple nursery rhymes. The patterns for "Hickory Dickory Dock," "Jack and Jill," and "Humpty Dumpty" are provided on pages 133-139.

Next, the puppeteer may retell a familiar folktale such as "The Elves and the Shoemaker," "Jack and the Beanstalk," or "The Town Mouse and the Country Mouse." The patterns for the puppets in these stories are included on pages 140-153. Students may wish to create scripts with dialogue, stage directions, acts, and scenes.

Puppeteers will want to create original stories with their own stick puppets. An example of an original play, "Harvest Awards," with appropriate puppets, is included on pages 156-158.

Ghost stories are especially stimulating for children. A "set" for a haunted house and patterns for a boy and a girl, are included on pages 160-162. Students may first use the script on page 159 for oral retell. The storytellers should draw their concept of the inside of the haunted house, using the blank form on page 161, and cover it with the picture of the outside of the house on page 160. The exterior will be removed at the end of the story. Later, students can use these models to create their own tale.

Even stick puppets can move to express a surprising variety of emotions. For example, a fearful puppet (say, a little pig confronted by a big, bad wolf) might quiver and shake or lean backward if the fear is sudden, or fall completely over in a faint. An excited character would probably jump up and down, a sad character would lean over forward. Students will discover this puppet language, or call upon experience for it, without being told outright.

(Text continues on page 154.)

Stage scene

Hickory

Dickory

Dock

Mouse

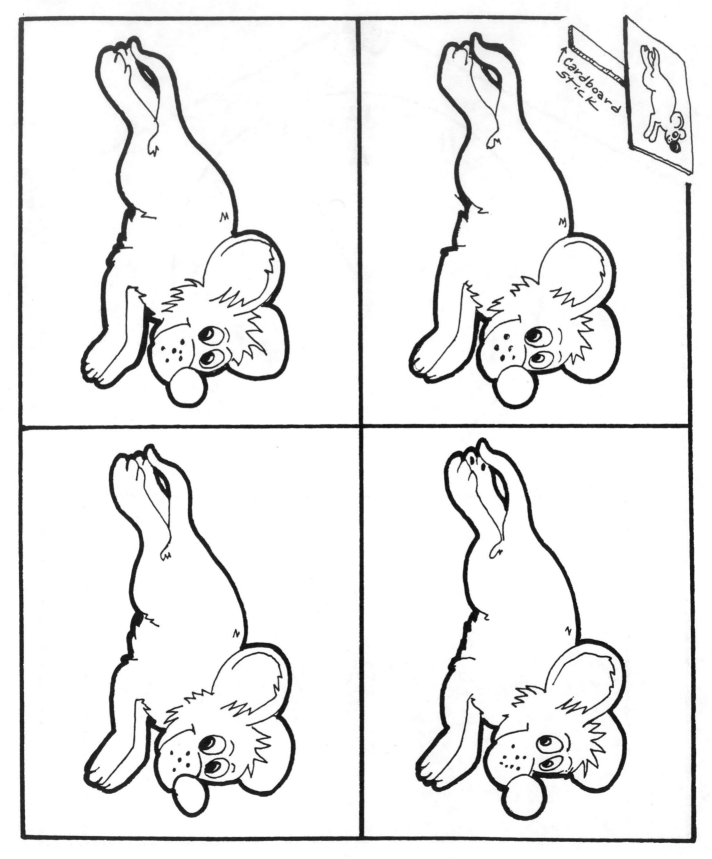

Stage scene

Jack

and

Jill

Jack and Jill

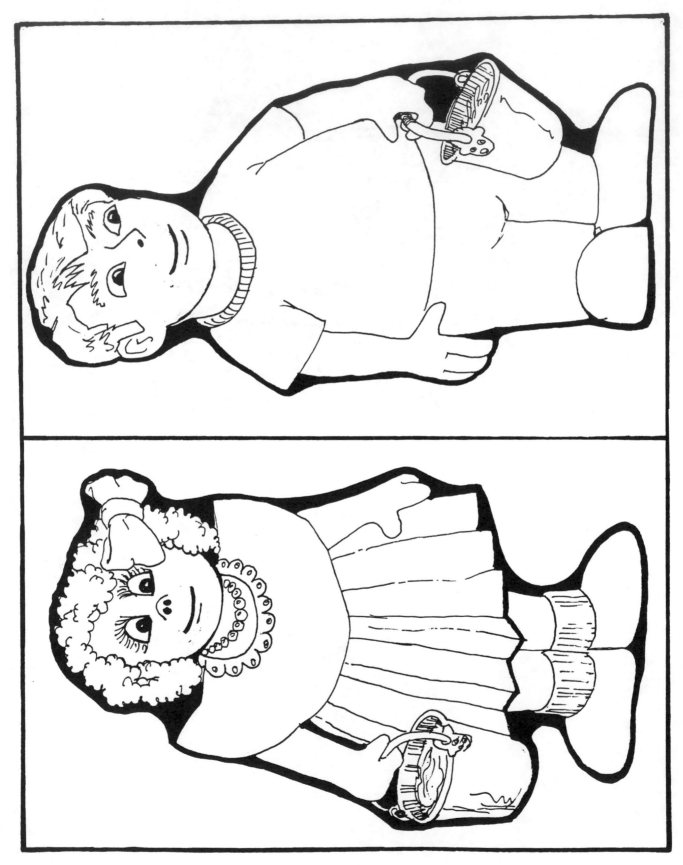

Stage scene

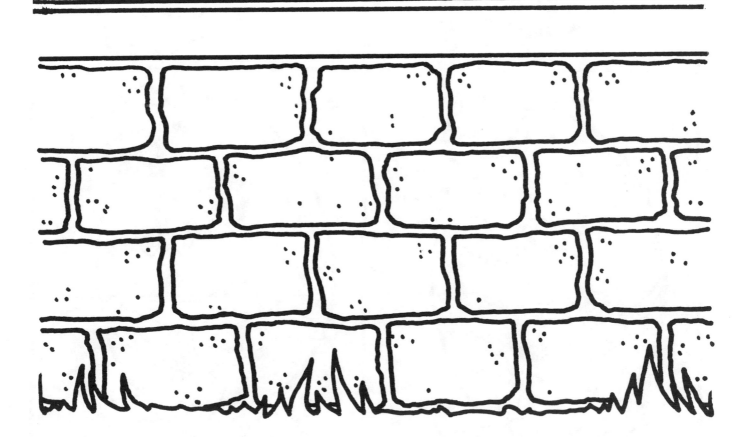

Humpty Dumpty

King's men and horses

Opening title

THE ELVES and the SHOEMAKER

PRESENTED BY

_____

Stage scene

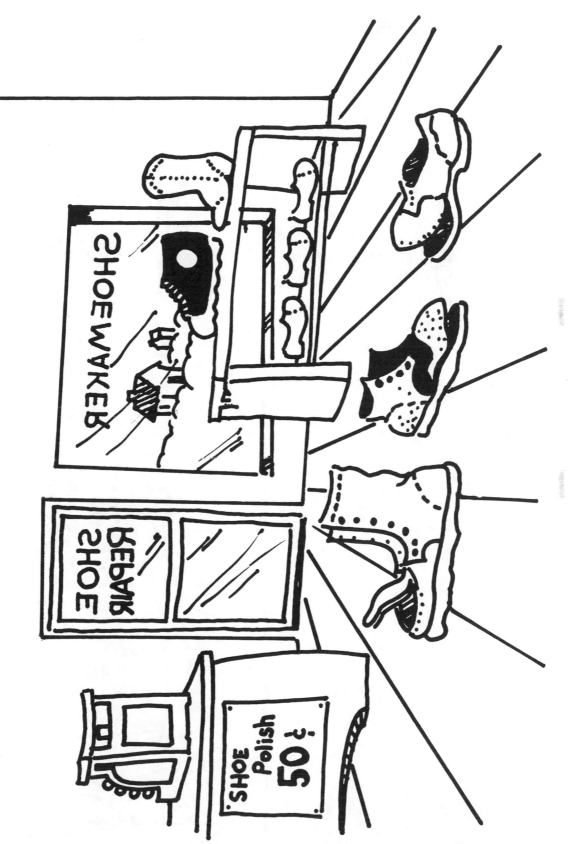

Shoemaker and wife

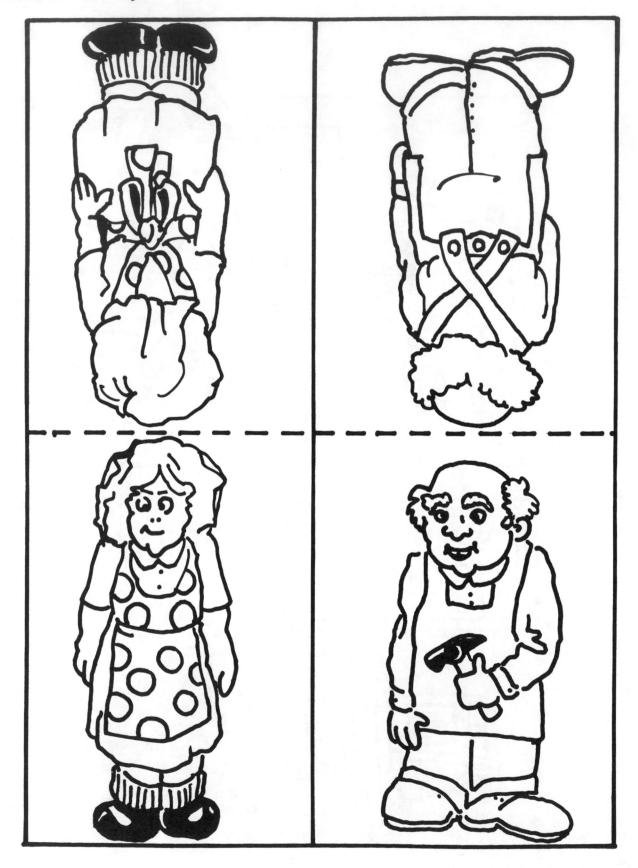

Elves

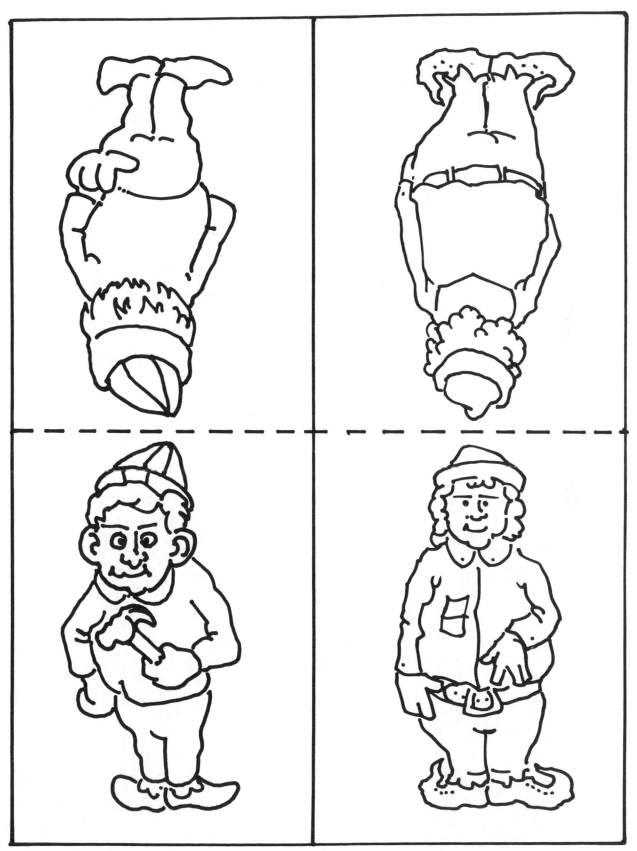

Customer

Opening title

JACK and the BEANSTALK

PRESENTED BY

_____

Stage scene (beanstalk)

Giant's wife, harp, and hen

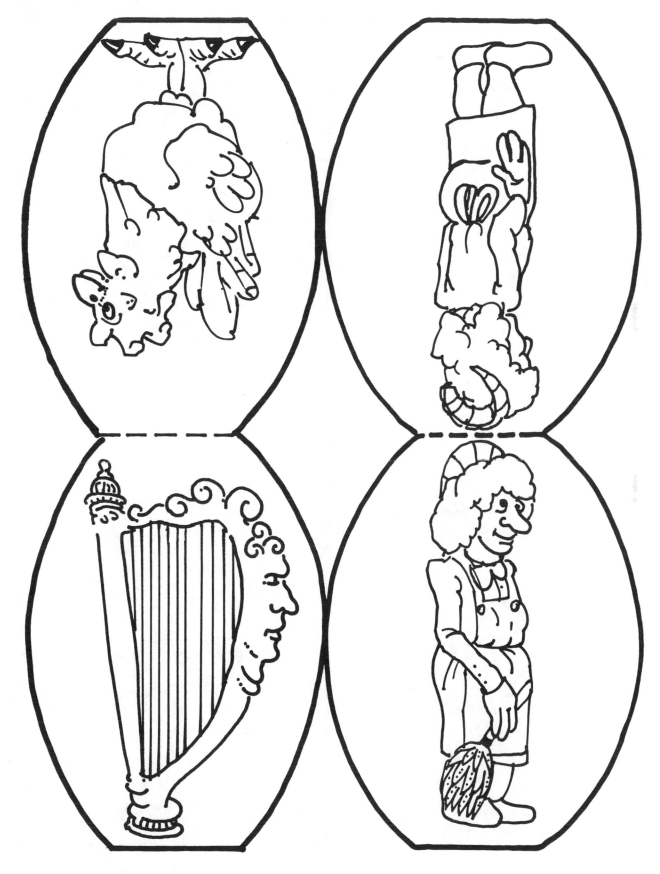

Jack and mother

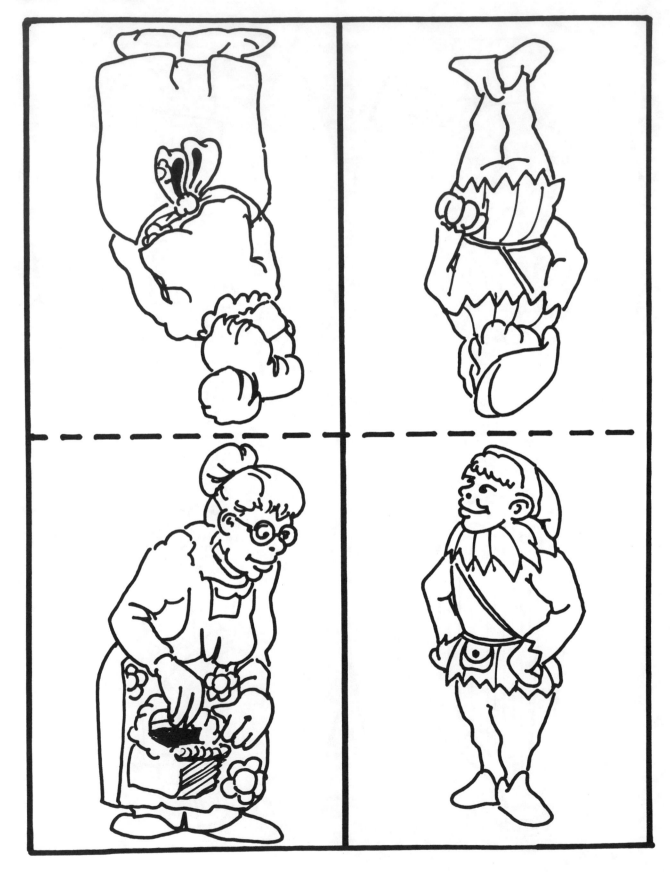

Opening title

The TOWN MOUSE and the COUNTRY MOUSE

PRESENTED BY

_____

Stage scene (town)

Cat

Harvest Awards
Harriet Kinghorn

[For one or more puppeteers]

PUPPETS: Farmer, Tomato, Carrot, Onion, Potato, Spinach, and Broccoli

SCENERY: Place the announcement of the awards on the cereal box stage. (The farmer is on-stage during the entire play. The puppets go on-stage as they are called up by the farmer during the play.)

FARMER: Hello, everyone. I'm happy to be here on this lovely fall day to give awards to the foods that I have grown in my garden this year. The fine harvest is gathered and I am thankful for it.

PUPPETS: Oh, this is so exciting!

FARMER: First of all, I would like to present Tomato, a fruit that is used as a vegetable, with a nutrition award for giving us vitamins A and C. Of course, we know that vitamin A helps us to have healthy skin and eyes and strong bones and teeth. And that vitamin C helps us to resist infections and is important for healthy blood vessels and bones. Congratulations, Tomato.

TOMATO: (blushing) I'm happy to get an award. Thank you.

FARMER: You're welcome. The next award will be presented to Carrot. Come right up here Carrot and receive your award for having a substance called carotene that becomes vitamin A in our bodies.

CARROT: I just don't know what to say except ... thanks a bunch!

FARMER: Isn't this a wonderful day? The next award goes to a vegetable that is not high in vitamins. But we really enjoy this vegetable because we use it in so many kinds of cooking. It is an honor for me to give Onion a special award for good taste.

ONION: O-O-O-h. Boo-hoo. O-O-O-h.

FARMER: Oh, dear, did I say something wrong? I didn't mean to hurt your feelings and make you cry, Onion.

ONION: I-I-I-I-m-m-m-m not crying because I'm sad. I'm crying because I'm happy.

FARMER: Whew, that's good. I was worried. I like "happy tears."

ONION: Thank you so-o-o much for my award.

FARMER: You're most welcome, Onion.

ONION: Oh, Boo-hoo. I'm so happy!

FARMER: The next member of the vegetable family to get an award is none other than Potato. It has vitamin C, which helps fight infections and helps make healthy gums, skin, blood vessels, and muscles. It also has vitamin B1 for steadying our nerves and vitamin B6 for helping make healthy bones. Yes, you are a great spud.

POTATO: Thank you. I'm pleased to be a helping spud.

FARMER: Green vegetables are certainly important to our health. The green vegetable that will receive an award today is Broccoli, which gives us vitamin B2, vitamin A, and vitamin C. Thank you, Broccoli, for your good nutrition.

BROCCOLI: Thank you ... thank you so much.

FARMER: The last award is for Spinach who gives us vitamin K, which helps to make our blood clot. It also provides vitamins A and B6.

SPINACH: Thank you. I'm proud of this award.

FARMER: Good, you should be proud of it. Thank you for coming, everyone. Thank you for coming to see our Harvest Awards presented on this fine day. Remember, children need the right vitamins to grow, and all of us need the right vitamins to stay healthy. Good-day, and stay healthy and happy with good nutrition.

(Text continues on page 159.)

Opening title

HARVEST AWARDS

AWARDS PRESENTED BY: _____

WHERE: _____

WHEN: _____

PUPPETEERS: _____

Harvest award characters

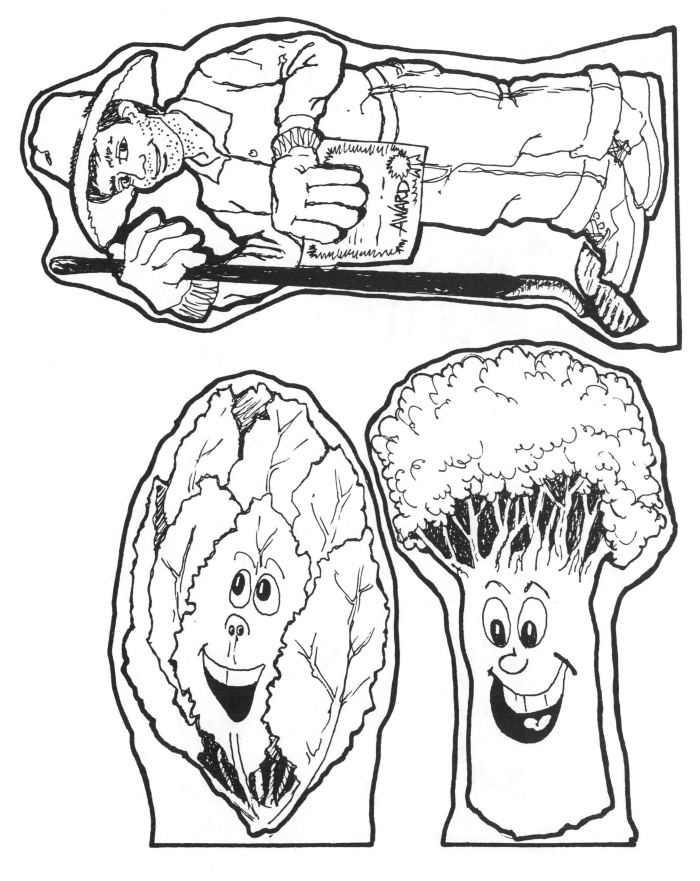

Harvest award characters

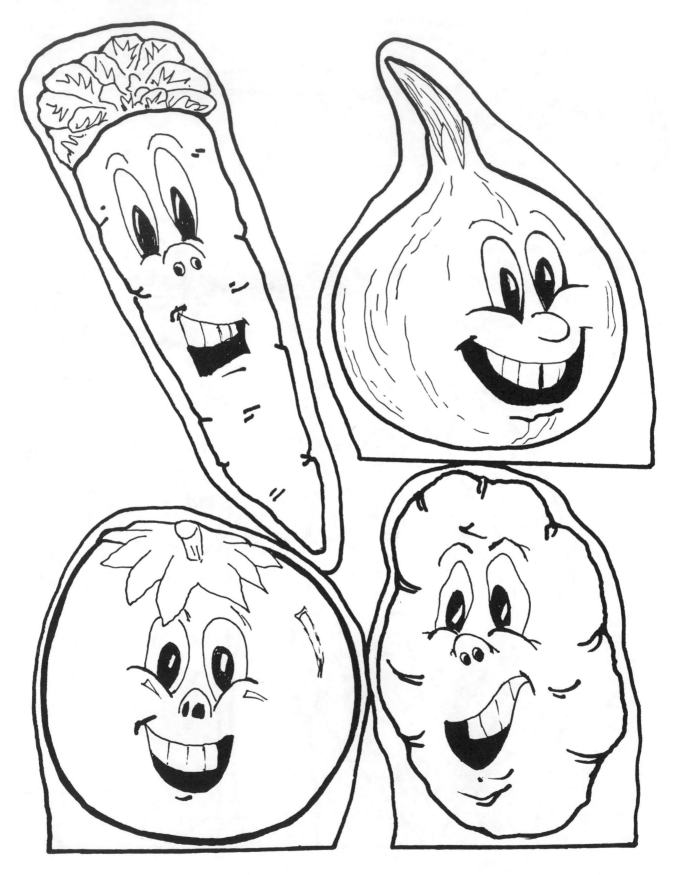

Is It Haunted?

Harriet Kinghorn

PREPARATION:	Sound effects person studies illustration of inside the house so that he or she knows what sounds to make for the play.
SCENERY:	Place the outside and inside of house in pocket, outside in front.
CHARACTERS:	Lori, Jack, and Sound Effects Person
LORI:	Have you ever been in a haunted house?
JACK:	No, and I'm not going in one.
LORI:	Me either. Some of my friends wanted me to go in a huanted house last year, but I didn't. I've always wondered what was inside, but I never have found out.
JACK:	Why didn't you ask your friends about what was inside?
LORI:	I did ask them, but they wouldn't tell me 'cause I wouldn't go in the house with them.
JACK:	Speaking of haunted houses, do you think that house over there is haunted?
LORI:	OH, it loo-o-oks haunted to me. Let's go just a little closer and listen for sounds from inside.
JACK:	Okay, but let's not get too close. [Children walk slowly toward house.]
SOUND EFFECTS PERSON:	[Make sounds that relate to the illustrations in house.]
LORI:	WOW! I guess it is haunted. I mean, it's HAUNTED!
JACK:	If I liked scary things, I'd go inside.
LORI:	Me too, but I don't even like scary things on TV.
JACK:	If we could only see what's inside the house without going inside, our problem would be solved.
LORI:	If I were a witch in a storybook, I could give us magic vision.
JACK:	Well, you're not a witch, so that's out. And I can do tricks, but not magic tricks, so that's out too.
LORI:	I have an idea! The next best thing to going inside is to "imagine" we're inside, right?
JACK:	I guess.
LORI:	Let's listen carefully. Then let's imagine what we think is inside. It will seem, well almost, like we are inside the house.
JACK:	Okay, I'll go along with that. Let's walk a little closer so we can hear better, then we'll tell what we think is inside.
SOUND EFFECTS PERSON:	[Make sounds that relate to the illustrations in house.]
LORI AND JACK:	[Tell about what they think they see inside the house.]
JACK:	That was fun. But I still wonder what really is inside that house.
LORI:	Me too. Are you thinking what I'm thinking?
JACK AND LORI:	Let's go in.
SOUND EFFECTS PERSON:	[Remove outside of house so everyone can see what's inside.]

(Text continues on page 163.)

Haunted house stage scene

Inside of house

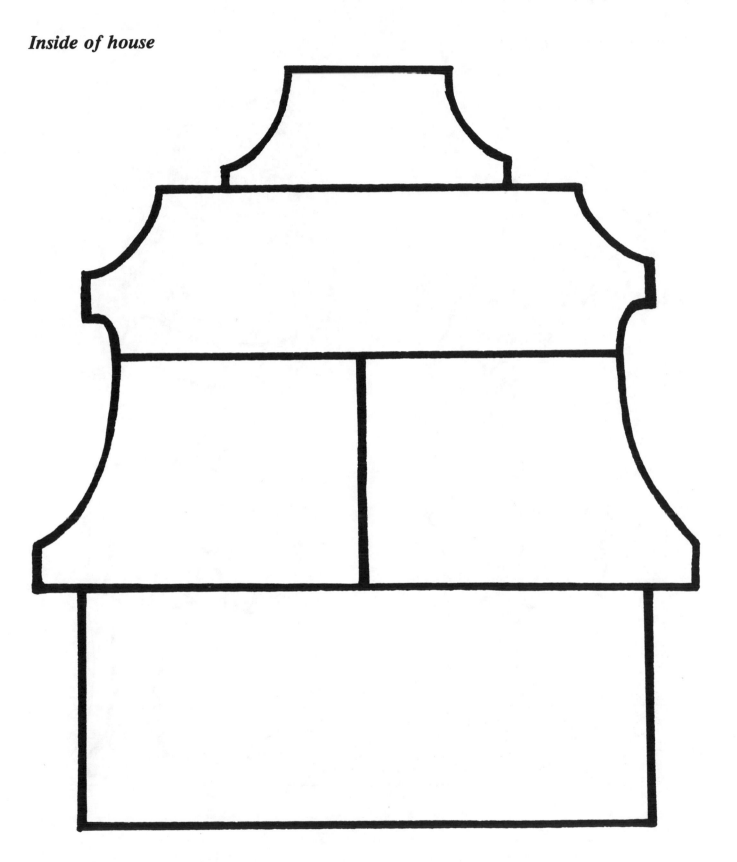

Haunted house characters

THREE-DIMENSIONAL PUPPETS

What creativity is unleashed when you put children and three-dimensional puppets together! A quick perusal of books on puppet theatres reveals a miracle of possible creations: bandana puppets, finger puppets, paper bag puppets, sock puppets, glove puppets, string puppets, box puppets, stuffed animal puppets, etc. Generally, three-dimensional puppets have the advantage of being able to move their hands, feet, and mouth and therefore are able to demonstrate a wider range of emotions. Students may wish to practice their puppets in front of a mirror so that they can explore conveying a variety of emotions, such as:

sadness	anger	uncertainty
joy	curiosity	shyness
fear	sleepiness	tenderness
surprise	repentance	bravery

Movement may need to be exaggerated to be interpreted by the audience; however, the puppeteer will need to be careful so that the movement does not detract from the story.

Students may wish to turn their old stuffed animals into puppets. In their excellent book *Storytelling with Puppets*, Nancy Renfro and Connie Champlin suggest the following methods for converting plush toys into puppets:

1. Cut a hole in the back of the toy's head and remove some stuffing to provide space for your hand. Consider slitting the mouth of the toy and sewing in a mouthpiece if the head area is large enough for a talking mouth.

2. Sew an inverted pocket on the back of the toy, removing enough stuffing to provide space for your hand or finger.

3. Cut a hole in the bottom of the toy, removing enough stuffing to provide space for your hand or finger.

4. Insert a wooden dowel to convert the toy into a simple rod puppet. Coat hanger wire or thin dowels could also be attached to the back of the toy's hands or arms, if loose jointed, to make it capable of additional movement. If this is done, some stuffing may need to be removed from the elbows or shoulder joints to facilitate smooth movement.

5. Attach strings to the arms and legs of dolls and animals to animate them for an impromptu marionette. Tape the strings to a cardboard tube control. (1985, 48)

After they have created their puppets and learned how to make them "come alive," students will develop their stories. Again, we recommend moving from simple to complex, starting with favorite folktales or books and later performing original puppet plays.

FLANNEL BOARDS

Flannel boards and the objects that go on them make fine aids that children can use for retelling stories from their textbooks, picture books, or from chapters in library books. After students become familiar with the flannel board, they might write their own stories and make their own objects to use with the board. They may wish to make themselves the main character in the story by using the patterns on page 165 and drawing their own face on the picture. To ensure that the pieces stick to the flannel board, put a strip of sandpaper, Velcro, or felt on the back.

Students might work with partners or in groups to present their flannel board stories in the following ways:

1. One child might place the objects on the flannel board while his or her partner retells a story or poem.

2. Two children might place objects on the board while other children present a choral reading.

3. Students might present their stories to other classes.

Flannel board stories can help children by developing comprehension, reinforcing vocabulary, and encouraging communication skills.

FLANNEL BOARD BOX

Children can make their own flannel board boxes to use both for storytelling and for storage of story characters. The directions follow.

Materials: Box with lid attached to one side, flannel, rubber cement or a fabric glue, and a piece of cardboard.

Directions: Cover the lid, which is attached to one side of the box, with flannel to make a flannel board box for storing flannel board materials and for telling flannel board stories. ("Ideal" boxes, which can be purchased in most school supply stores, are excellent.)

Cut a piece of cardboard approximately three inches wide and as long as needed to hold the lid on the box up at a slight slant.

Children of all ages will enjoy using these flannel board boxes over and over again for retelling their favorite stories at school and at home. Although children can make some of their own flannel board materials, they will also enjoy using commercial products. See bibliography for sources of commercial materials.

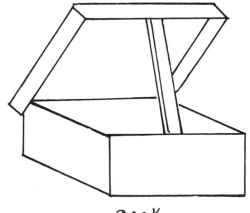

Back

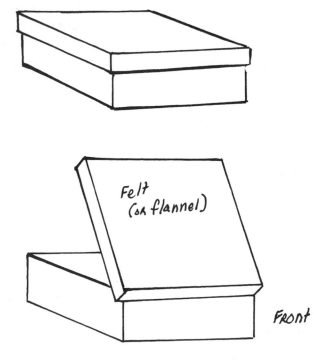

Felt (or flannel)

Front

Flannel board characters

BIBLIOGRAPHY

Flannel Board or One-Dimensional Puppets

Kinghorn, Harriet, and Robert King. *Storytime Classics—The Big Lion and the Little Mouse*. Minneapolis: T. S. Denison, 1987. Pre-K to 3. (All the Kinghorn and King books include a story, puppet patterns, and flannel board patterns.)

_____. *Storytime Classics—The Hungry Day (The Gingerbread Man)*. Minneapolis: T. S. Denison, 1987. Pre-K to 3.

_____. *Storytime Classics—The Little Red Hen*. Minneapolis: T. S. Denison, 1987. Pre-K to 3.

_____. *Storytime Classics—Red Riding Hood*. Minneapolis: T. S. Denison, 1988. Pre-K to 3.

_____. *Storytime Classics—The Three Bears*. Minneapolis: T. S. Denison, 1988. Pre-K to 3.

_____. *Storytime Classics—The Three Goats*. Minneapolis: T. S. Denison, 1987. Pre-K to 3.

_____. *Storytime Classics—The Three Pigs*. Minneapolis: T. S. Denison, 1987. Pre-K to 3.

_____. *Storytime Classics—The Tortoise and the Hare*. Minneapolis: T. S. Denison, 1987. Pre-K to 3.

Noel, Karen. *Cut and Color, Book I—Family, Friends and Feelings*. Minneapolis: T. S. Denison, 1985. Pre-K to 1.

_____. *Cut and Color, Book II—Learning Concepts*. Minneapolis: T. S. Denison, 1985. Pre-K to 1.

_____. *Cut and Color, Book III—Holidays and Special Times*. Minneapolis: T. S. Denison, 1985. Pre-K to 1.

Scott, Louise B. *All That Fuss for Nothing*. File Folder Fables/Folk Tales. Six in Series. (Based upon Aesop and other tales.) Minneapolis: T. S. Denison, 1988. Pre-K to 3.

_____. *The Dog and the Bone*. File Folder Fables/Folk Tales. Minneapolis: T. S. Denison, 1988. Pre-K to 3.

_____. *How the Skunk Got Its Stripe*. File Folder Fables/Folk Tales. Minneapolis: T. S. Denison, 1988. Pre-K to 3.

_____. *Why the Raccoon Has a Mask*. File Folder Fables/Folk Tales. Minneapolis: T. S. Denison, 1988. Pre-K to 3.

_____. *Why the Shark Swims in the Sea*. File Folder Fables/Folk Tales. Minneapolis: T. S. Denison, 1988. Pre-K to 3.

Puppets

Frazier, Nancy, and Nancy Renfro. *Imagination: At Play with Puppets and Creative Drama*. Austin, Tex.: Nancy Renfro Studios, 1987.

Renfro, Nancy, and Connie Champlin. *Storytelling with Puppets*. Chicago: American Library Association, 1985.

Wright, Denise Anton. *One-Person Puppet Plays*. Englewood, Colo.: Libraries Unlimited, 1990.

9 Storytelling Crafts

Although storytelling is an oral tradition, children's imaginations can be stimulated by connecting storytelling with visual and manipulative materials. This chapter includes a variety of crafts that can be used in conjunction with storytelling. Through the use of crafts, students learn a number of things:

- There is more than one way to tell a story.

- Simple props and costumes can be made from almost anything.

- Creating craft props for storytelling can aid in story creation, story memory, and audience appeal.

- Creating crafts and stories is just plain fun.

Once children become aware of their creative power, they become limitless people. Within everything is a story. They just have to find it and "let it out." Although we encourage students to create original crafts and stories, we have included a number of patterns for those who wish to use them to get started. The crafts in this chapter were designed by Harriet Kinghorn.

MISCELLANEOUS CRAFT IDEAS

Lighthouse

Materials: Small paper plate, 9" x 12" construction paper, yellow paper (slightly smaller than construction paper), black tempera paint, and brushes, markers, or crayons

Preparations: Cut out a circle (approximately 7½ centimeters in diameter) inside each paper plate (for younger children who might need help). If paint is used, prepare painting work area.

cut hole in plate.

slip it over rolled Construction Paper.

Directions:

1. Read about real lighthouses.
2. Cut out a circle inside the paper plate to hold the construction paper for the lighthouse (if not already done).
3. Paint the paper plate on both sides. Let it dry.
4. Use markers or crayons to draw details on lighthouse, such as windows and door on lower part. Cut rectangles in the construction paper to represent windows.
5. Roll up the paper and place the top of the paper inside the paper plate.
6. Roll up the yellow paper. Insert it inside the full length of the lighthouse to represent a light.

Storytelling: Write or tell a story about how your lighthouse feels, who the lighthouse sees, and the people the lighthouse helps.

Opossum

Materials: Book about opossums, construction paper, scissors, chenille type pipe cleaners, reinforcement ring, and crayons or markers

Preparation: If long chenille sticks are used, cut them in half.

Directions:

1. Read about opossums.

2. Fold a piece of paper in half. Draw an outline of half the opossum. Then cut out the outline and unfold the paper for a whole opossum.

3. Color the opossum to make it look furry.

4. Color the reinforcement ring approximately the same color as the opossum. Place it where the tail belongs.

5. Poke the pipe cleaner through the hole of the reinforcement ring.

6. Bend the opossum's pipe cleaner tail around your finger to hold and carry it when you tell a story.

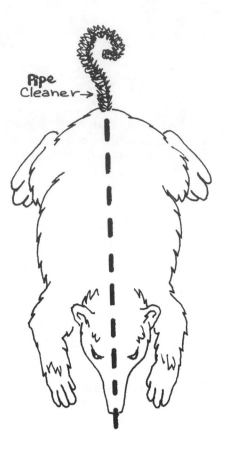

Storytelling: Create and tell or write a story about an opossum. It can be a nonfiction or fiction story. It might be a story about why the opossum plays possum.

Houseboat

Materials: Books about houseboats, a small milk carton, a small plastic plate, construction paper for sides and roof of the houseboat, crayons or markers, glue, scissors, a dishpan, and a large ice cream pail or sink filled with water (to float the houseboat)

Preparation: For younger children, cut the siding and roof from construction paper on a paper cutter. Older children can measure their own houseboats and paper.

Directions:

1. Read about houseboats.

2. Cut out and glue the paper siding on the milk carton.

3. Decorate the house with crayons or markers.

4. Cut out and glue on the roof.

5. Place the house on a plastic plate and then float the houseboat in water.

Storytelling: Create a story about where your houseboat goes, what it sees, and what adventures it has.

Pancake

Materials: Cardboard pizza circle (or a paper plate), spool, glue, brown tempera paint, and scraps of construction paper

Preparation: Cover the tables with newspaper. Set out paint and brushes (small milk cartons make excellent paint containers).

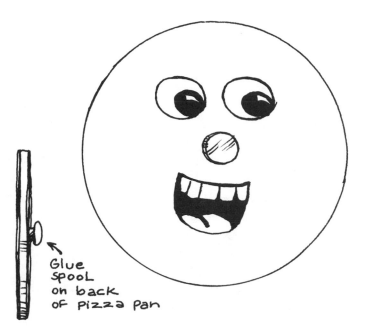

Glue spool on back of pizza pan

Directions:

1. Paint a pizza circle to represent a pancake.

2. Cut out facial features from scraps of paper and glue them on the circle.

3. Glue a spool on the back of the circle to serve as a handle.

Storytelling: Create and tell a story about a pancake, using the pancake you made.

Tote
(For a Nature Walk Story)

Materals: A paper sandwich bag for each person, a tagboard strip for a handle (optional), glue, crayons, and markers

Preparation: See that each child has the proper materials to make a nature bag. Make plans for the time and place of the nature walk.

Directions:

1. Decorate a bag with your name and designs or pictures. Then glue on a handle to make a tote bag to take on a nature walk.

2. Discuss the many things you might see on a nature walk.

3. Go on the nature walk and put a few items in your bag, such as a blade of grass, various kinds of leaves, and a small twig.

4. After you return from your walk, prepare a story about your walk. What did you see, touch, smell, hear, and taste on your walk? How did the walk make you feel? What did you observe on your walk that you had not noticed before. (Show the items in your bag.)

5. As you tell your story, you might put each item back in your bag after you've told about it.

Stand-Up Storybook

Materials: A piece of construction paper for a cover; chenille sticks, yarn, or string for a handle; writing or drawing paper for the pages inside the book; crayons or markers; pencil; reinforcement rings; paper punch; and staplers

Preparation: Make booklets for younger children. Older children can make their own. Cut the string for the booklets.

Directions:

1. Fold the writing paper in half and staple it together near the fold to use as the pages of the booklet. Then attach the cover.

2. Punch two holes near the fold of the booklet where the handle will go. Reinforce these holes with reinforcement rings.

3. Attach a handle to the booklet.

4. Create and write a story.

5. Decorate the front cover to represent the first part of your story, and decorate the back cover to represent the end of your story.

Storytelling: Stand your book up to show your listeners the front cover of your booklet when you tell your story. At the end of the story, turn your booklet so the listeners can see a picture of the ending. You may even have your picture tell the ending.

Front

Back

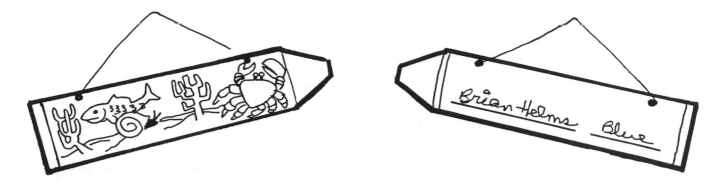

Crayon

Materials: Crayons, tagboard or construction paper, various colors of yarn, a stapler, and the pattern in this section

Preparation: Cut yarn to desired lengths for crayon handles.

Directions:

1. Use only one crayon to design a monochromatic picture on one side of a tagboard crayon. (If yarn is used, a crayon and yarn handle can match in color.)

2. In the same color write your own name on the opposite side of the crayon to show who owns it. For example, Brian can print, "Brian Helms" on his crayon.

Storytelling: Create and write and/or tell a story about an exciting adventure with a crayon, or another kind of story about a crayon. It can be a realistic or imaginary story.

Crayon pattern

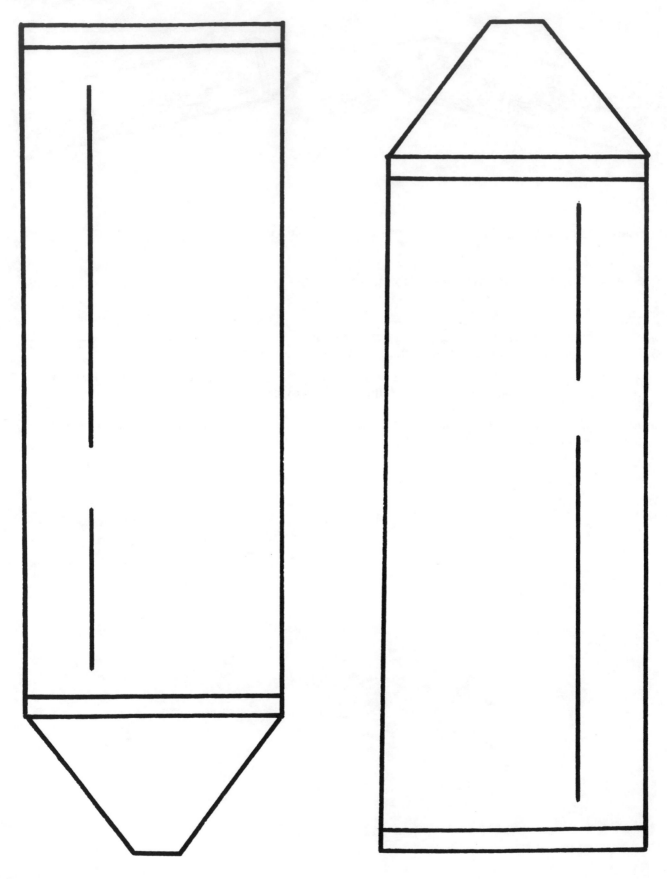

Magnet

Materials: Paper, crayons, pencil, scissors, a tagboard magnet, a real magnet, and glue

Preparation: Reproduce magnets for each student from the pattern provided on the following page.

Directions:

1. Color and cut out the magnet.

2. Look for materials that will adhere to a magnet and find some. Make a list of the items that adhered to the real magnet.

3. Make pictures of the items that adhered to the magnet and glue them to the tagboard magnet.

Variation: A piece of magnetic tape can be glued to the bottom of each side of the tagboard magnets so that each student has his or her own magnet.

Storytelling: Tell a story about your experiences on your magnetic search. What items did you think might adhere to a magnet, but didn't? You might tell what you wondered about on your walk to find things that would adhere to your magnet. Which item seemed to adhere best? Tell why. Students might also make up a creative "How and Why Tale" about how magnets came to be.

Creative Junk Craft

Materials: Throwaway items such as lids, paper and plastic plates, spools, yarn, wallpaper, plastic jars, paper bags, tubes, cups, etc., and a box to hold throwaways

Preparation: Collect throwaway items over a period of time.

Directions:

1. Choose three or four items of junk, make a list of all the things you could make out of those pieces of junk, and make one item.

2. After you have created your item, write and tell a realistic or imaginary story about your creative craft.

3. Make a sketch or picture of your junk craft.

Magnet pattern

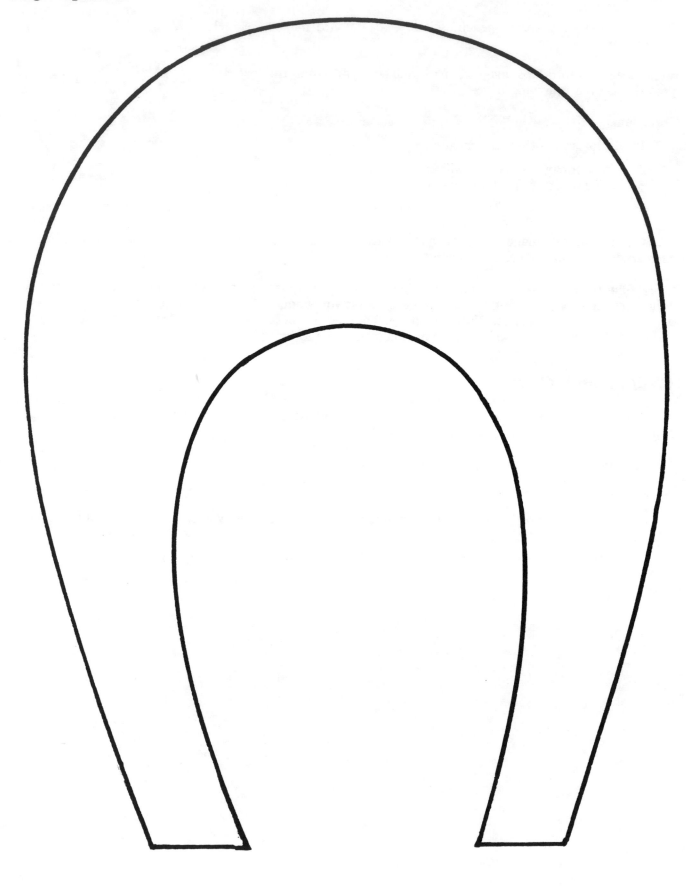

Creative Writing and Storytelling Booklet

We saw this booklet made by Carol Elsholz at the Bill Martin Workshop in Grand Forks, North Dakota, and she gave us permission to share it here.

Materials: Paper, any size masking tape, scissors, and table

Directions:

1. Place a sheet of paper lengthwise in front of you on a table.
2. Put a piece of masking tape halfway on the sheet of paper and halfway on the table as seen in the illustration. Continue this process with as many other sheets of paper as you want in the booklet.
3. Pick the sheets up from the table and fold the tape over the back sheet to bind the booklet.
4. Cut off the extra tape on each edge.
5. Show the children how to make these booklets for creative writing and for storytelling projects.

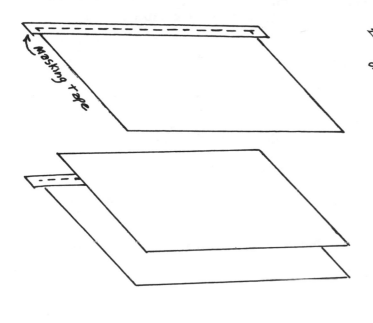

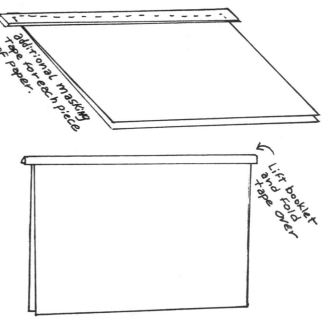

SIT-UPS

Sit-ups are simple paper toys that are cut out and folded to sit on a shelf, desk, or windowsill as props for storytelling. The storyteller should select a character from those shown on pages 177-179, or design their own sit-up character, and then create a story to go with the character. Kinghorn's story that follows is an example of a story that children may use with sit-up characters. First, the student cuts out and folds the rabbit and the lion shown on pages 177 and 178. Then the teller places the characters in the appropriate position on the classroom bookshelf and retells the story in his or her own words. Sit-ups, like puppets or flannel boards, are one more way to tie the oral telling of a story with a simple visual prop.

Jane's Sit-Ups
Harriet Kinghorn

"Why, me? Why is it always me that has to sit on the bottom shelf of the toy cabinet?" asked Rabbit. "I get tired of looking at shoes and mop heads and broom bristles."

"Gr-r-r," answered Lion, who happened to be sitting on the top shelf, "I guess Jane thinks that this is the way we toys look best on the shelves."

"Maybe Jane thinks we look best this way, but I don't. I'm tired of sitting on the bottom shelf year after year, month after month, week after week, day after day, hour after hour, minute after minute, and moment af...."

"Gr-r-r. I get the point," roared Lion. "I would like to change places with you from time to time, but since we can't move by ourselves, we'll just have to make the best of it."

Just then Jane and her friend, Kim, came hurrying into the room. "I told Mom that I would dust my toy shelf before I go to the park," Jane said.

"I'll help. Then we can go to the park sooner," said Kim.

"Great! You can take this feather duster and dust the shelves where the paper sit-ups are sitting. I'll pick up these toys over here."

"Okay," said Kim.

"Oh boy!" thought Rabbit. "This might be my chance to move up!" Kim took off the sit-ups, dusted the shelves and put most of the sit-ups back in the same places.

"Well," said Rabbit. "I guess I'll be sitting here the rest of my day ... ay...!" Right then, Rabbit found himself zooming through the air. He landed on the top shelf exactly in the spot where he had been wanting to sit for a long time.

"I think you belong on this top shelf, Rabbit. You need a little more space for your long lean ears," said Kim. "I like your paper sit-ups, Jane. I think I'll make some to put on my bookshelf."

"They're fun to make," said Jane. "Are you ready to go to the park?"

"Sure, let's go."

As soon as the girls left the room, Rabbit shouted, "I finally made it to the top! It's wonderful looking at *people's* heads rather than dusty *mop* heads. I can see the top of the table rather than just underneath it."

"I'm certainly glad that you made it to the top," said Lion, who was now sitting on the bottom shelf."

Rabbit looked down to the lowest shelf to talk to Lion.

"Thanks, Lion, I am too ... oo ... ooo."

"What's the matter, Rabbit?" asked Lion.

"Oh, I feel so strange when I look down at you," answered Rabbit, now looking straight ahead. "I nearly fell off the shelf when I looked down to talk to you. Did you ever feel that way when you looked down at me when I was down there?"

"No, looking down didn't bother me, but it does bother some characters. It's called vertigo when that happens."

"Well, I'll just make the best of it. I'll never look down, again." Rabbit felt frightened sitting on the top shelf but he didn't want the other sit-ups to know how he felt, especially since he had talked so much about wanting to move up to the top.

"Hi, sit-ups," said Jane, as she came into the room. "Kim and I had a great time at the park. You all look fine the way Kim arranged you on the shelves, except for one of you. Rabbit, you look lonely up there. I know where you belong."

"Oh, no!" thought Rabbit, as he was being carried from one shelf to another. "Just when I finally made it to the top, Jane is moving me back down to the bottom shelf. The top shelf isn't perfect, but I can hardly bear to think about seeing mostly grungy sneakers, dusty mop heads, and dirty broom bristles, again."

Jane put Rabbit down and then said, "Rabbit, you look just right here on the middle shelf." Then she skipped out of the room.

"Oh," said Rabbit looking all around. "This is the best place to be, for it's not too high and it's not too low. It's just right."

"Gr ... rr ... eat!" roared Lion.

(Text continues on page 180.)

Toy sit-ups

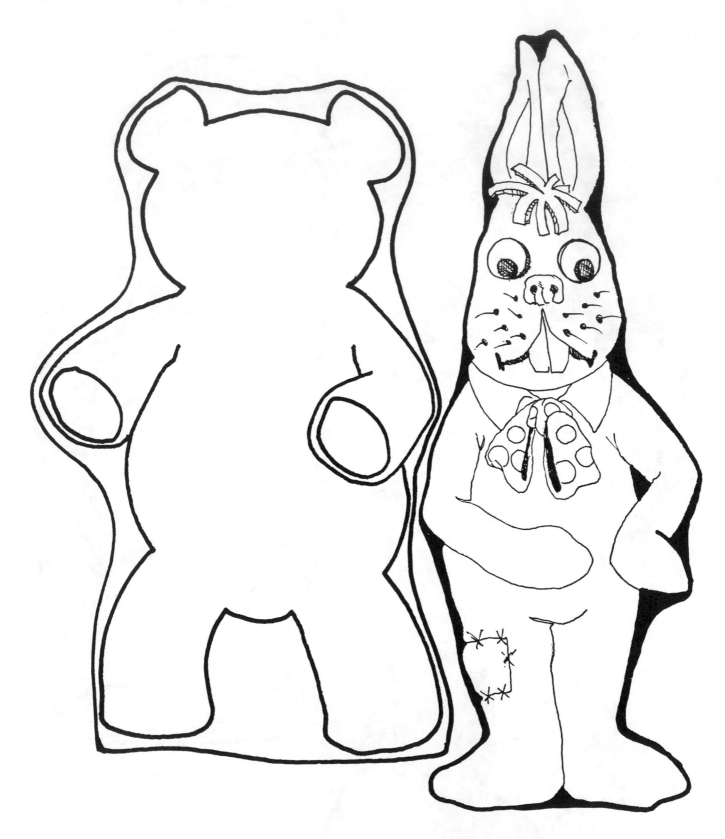

HATS, FACES, AND HEADPIECES

Create stories about one or more of the hats, faces, or headpieces in this section, or make a hat or headpiece of your own to write and/or tell a story about. Patterns follow.

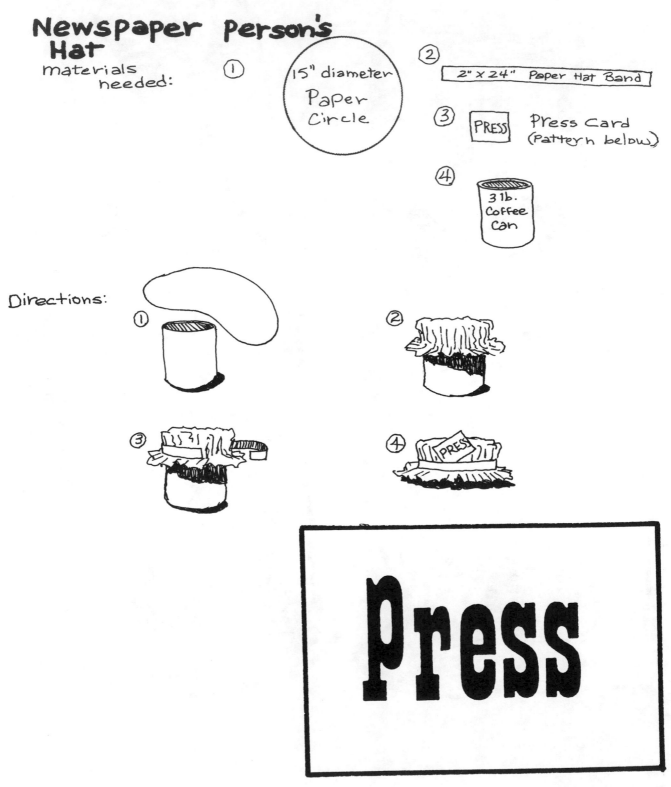

Newspaper Person's Hat

materials needed:

① 15" diameter Paper Circle

② 2" x 24" Paper Hat Band

③ PRESS Press Card (Pattern below)

④ 3 lb. Coffee Can

Directions:

①

②

③

④

Press

(Text continues on page 196.)

Police hat

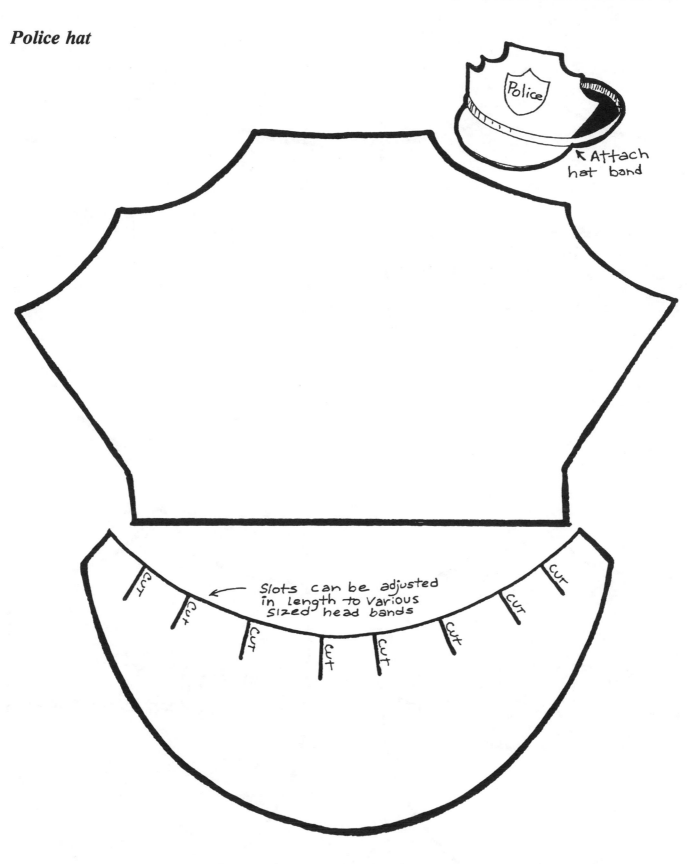

Attach hat band

Slots can be adjusted in length to various sized head bands

CUT

Badges

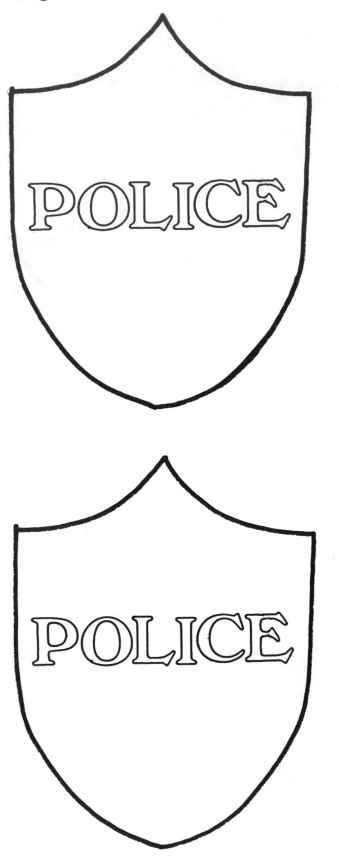
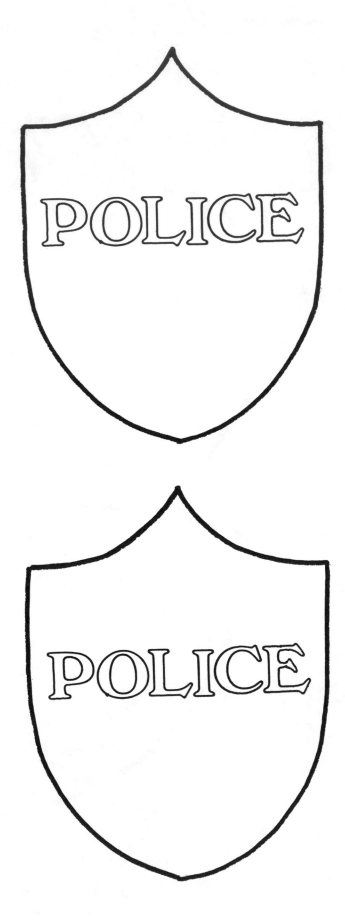

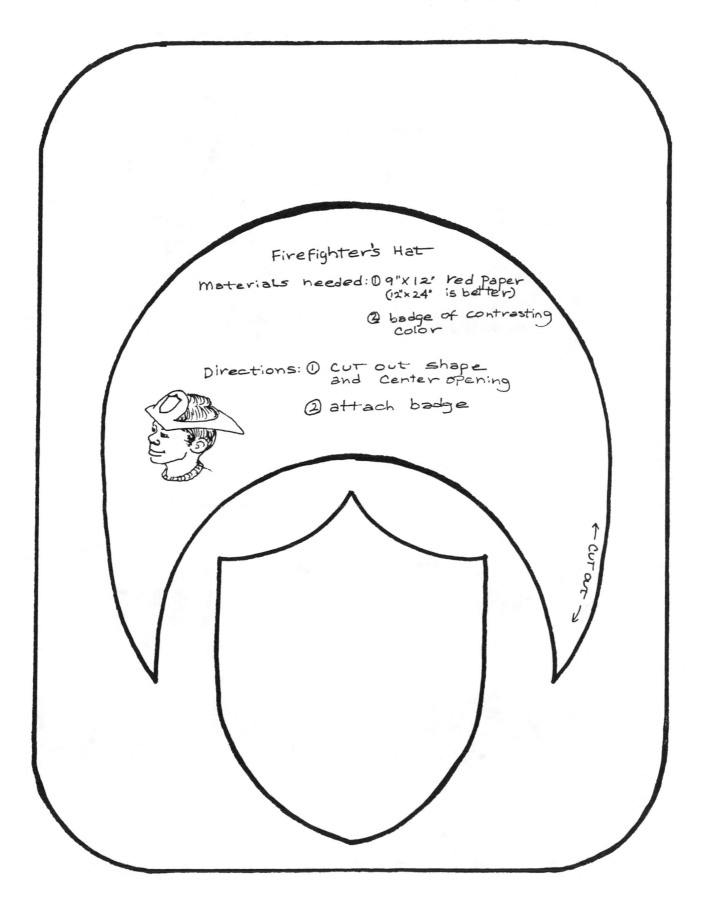

Firefighter's Hat

Materials needed: ① 9"x 12' red Paper
(12"x 24' is better)

② badge of contrasting
color

Directions: ① cut out shape
and center opening

② attach badge

← CUT OUT →

Badges

Nurse's hat

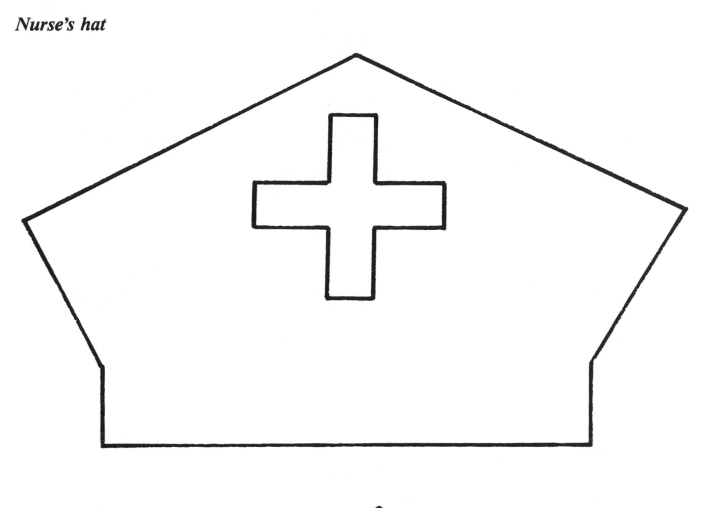

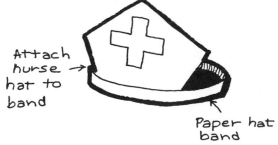

Attach nurse hat to band

Paper hat band

Rabbit ears

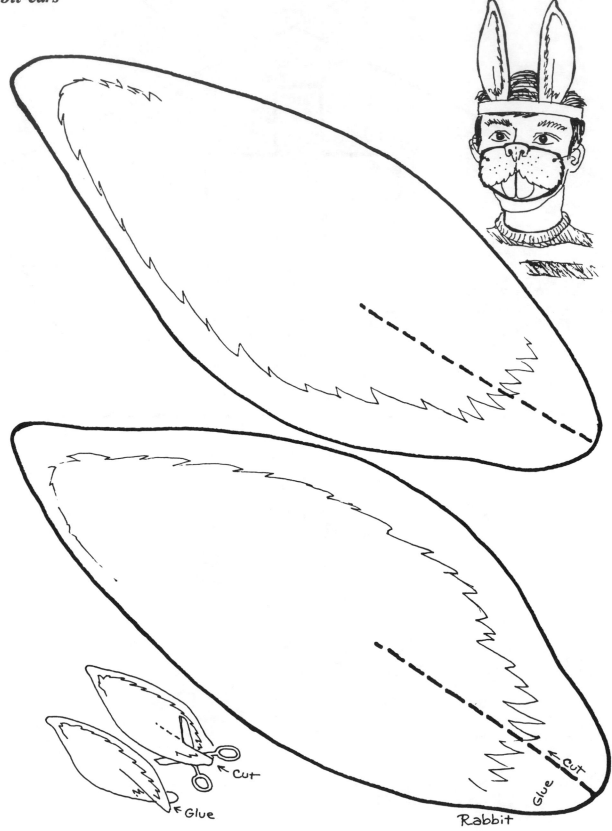

Cut

Glue

Cut

Glue

Rabbit

Rabbit nose

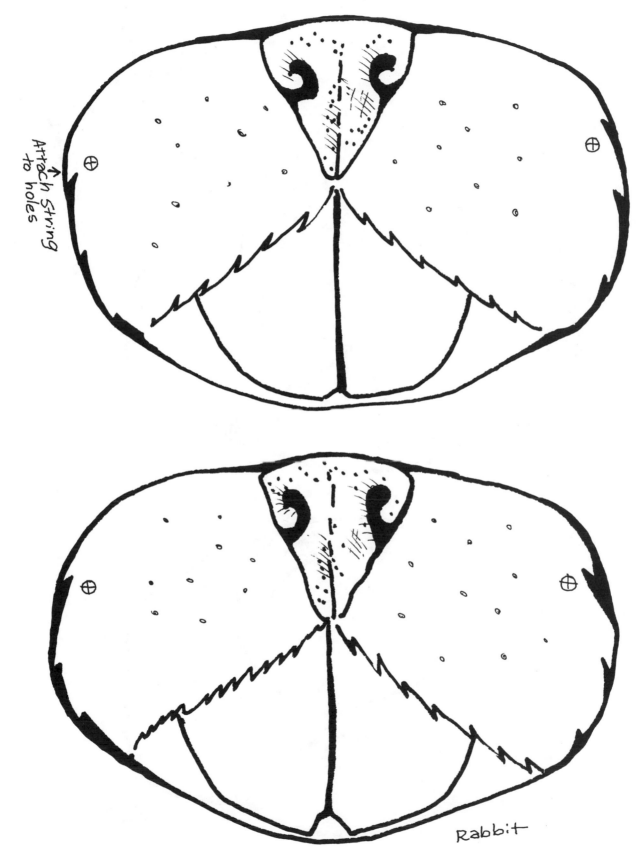

Attach string to holes

Rabbit

Mouse nose

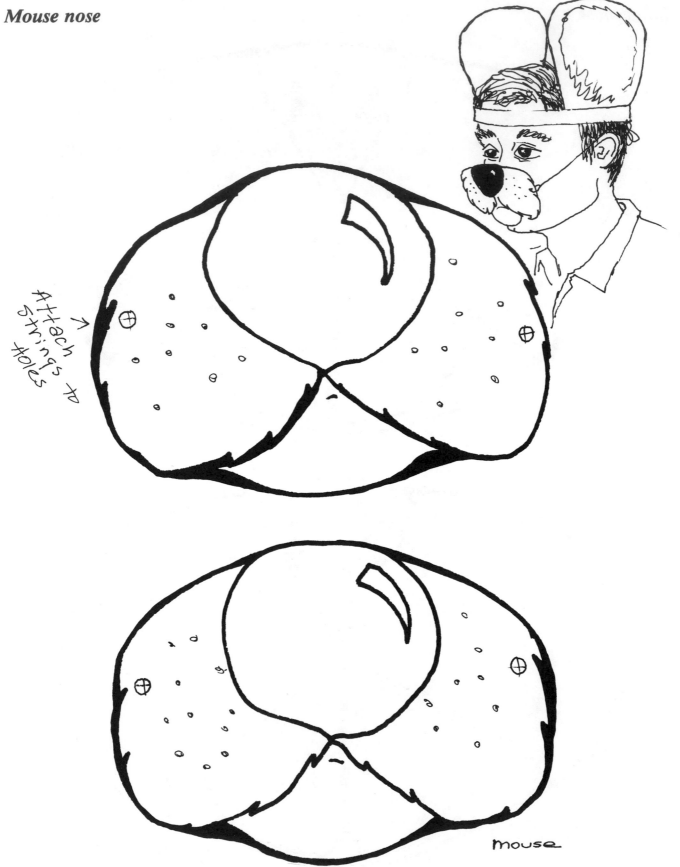

Attach strings to holes

mouse

Mouse ears

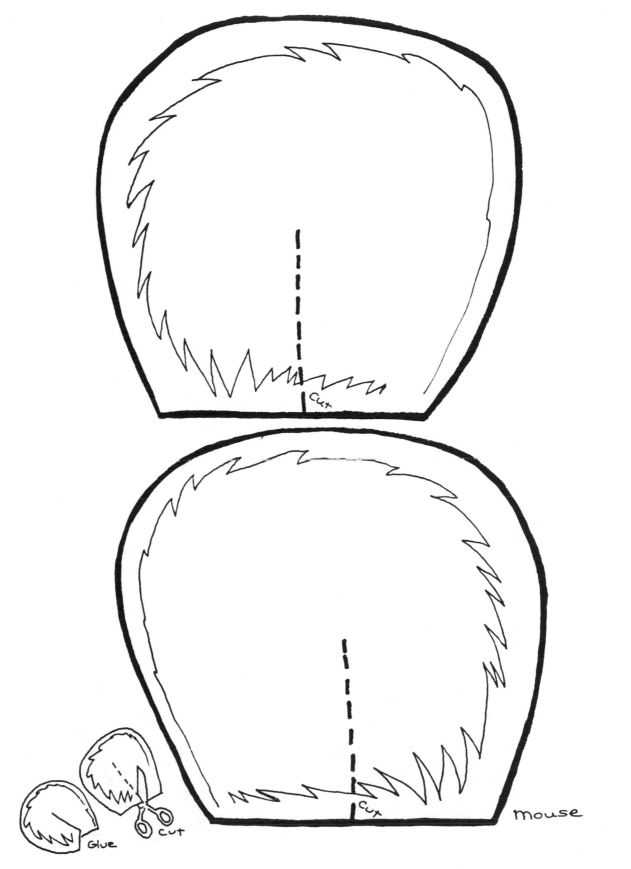

Mouse

Cat ears

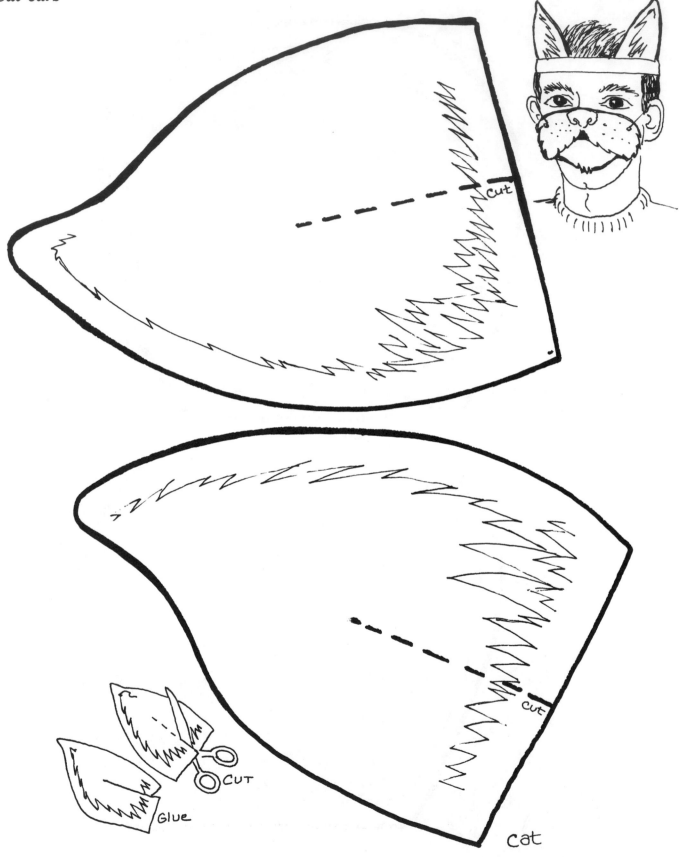

Cat nose

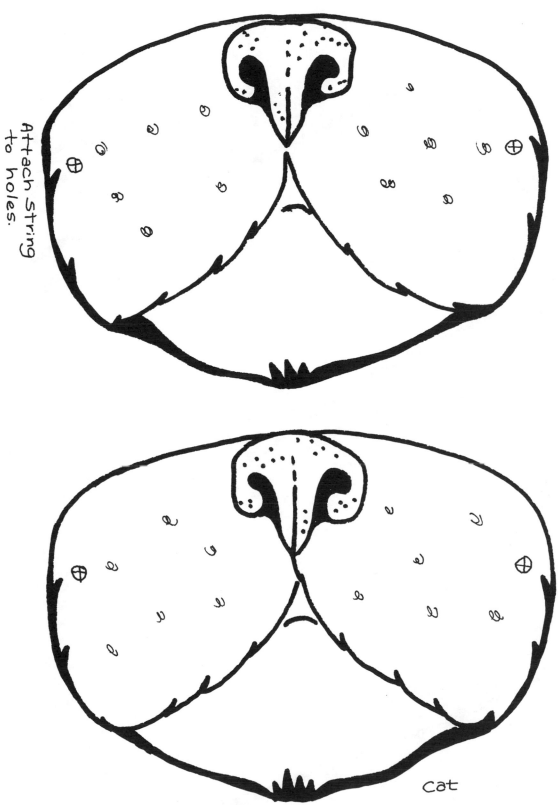

Attach string to holes.

cat

Dog ears

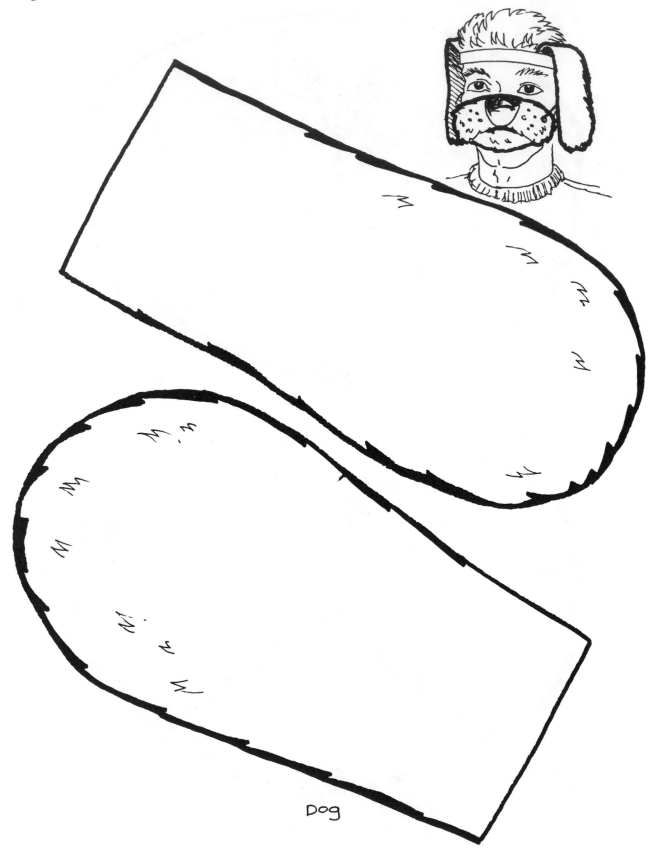

Dog

Dog nose

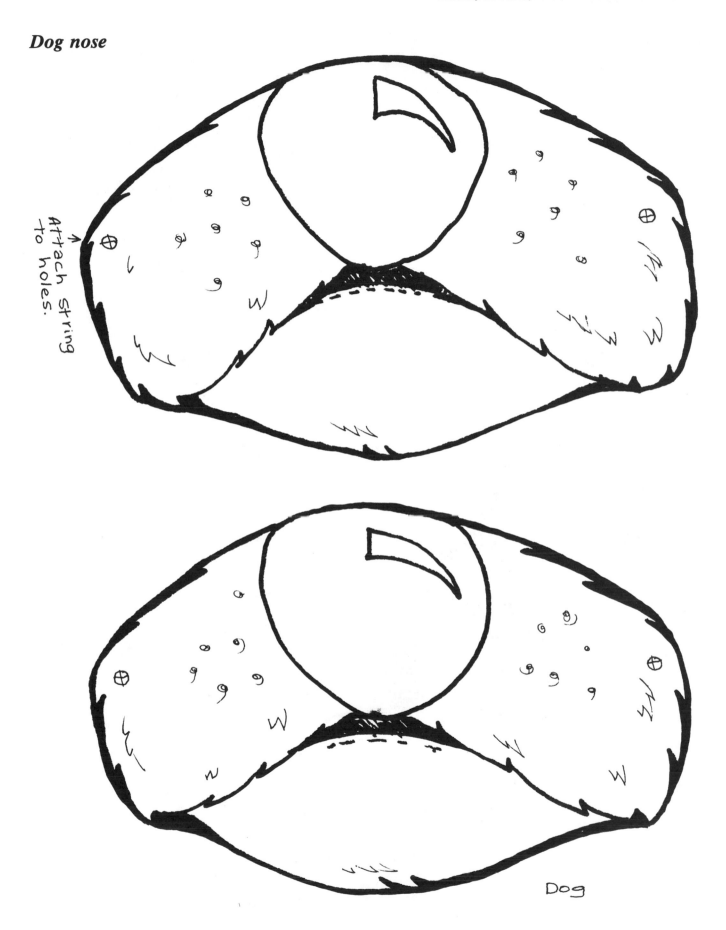

Attach string to holes.

Dog

Elephant nose

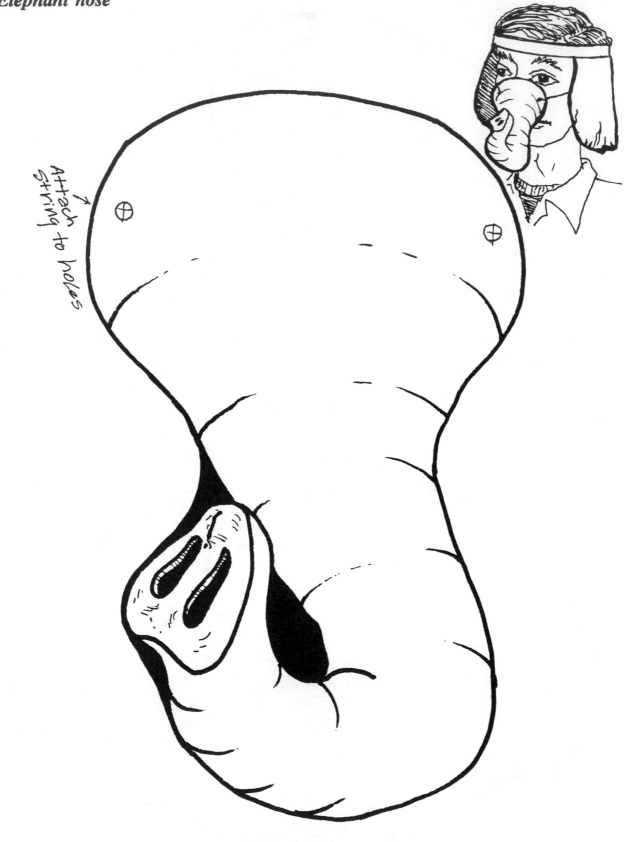

Attach string to holes

Elephant ears

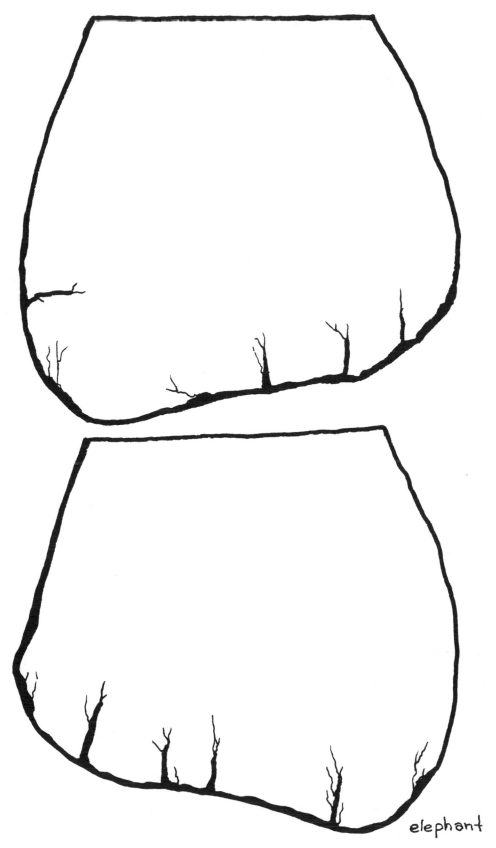

elephant

BIBLIOGRAPHY

Behrens, June. *I Can Be a Nurse*. Chicago: Children's Press, 1986.

Blos, Joan W. *Martin's Hat*. Illustrated by Marc Simont. New York: Morrow, 1984. (Fiction)

Broekel, Ray. *I Can Be an Author*. Chicago: Children's Press, 1986. (Books)

Broger, Achim. *Francie's Paper Puppy*. Illustrated by Michelle Sambin. Natrick, Mass.: Picture Book Studio, 1984. (Dog sit-up)

Christelow, Eileen. *Mr. Murphy's Marvelous Invention*. New York: Clarion, 1983. (Junk craft)

Connolly, James E. *Why the Possum's Tail Is Bare*. Illustrated by Andrea Adams. Owings Mills, Md.: Stemmer House, 1985. (Possum craft)

Fitz-Gerald, Christine. *I Can Be a Reporter*. Chicago: Children's Press, 1986.

Fitzpatrick, Julie. *Magnets*. Morristown, N.J.: Silver Burdette, 1984. (Magnet craft)

Gelman, Rita Golden. *Hello Cat You Need a Hat*. New York: Scholastic, 1979. (Fiction)

Geringer, Laura. *A Three Hat Day*. Illustrated by Arnold Lobel. New York: Harper and Row, 1985. (Fiction)

Goodall, John S. *Paddy's New Hat*. New York: Atheneum, 1980. (Fiction)

Hankin, Rebecca. *I Can Be a Fire Fighter*. Chicago: Children's Press, 1985.

Henkes, Kevin. *Once around the Block*. Illustrated by Victoria Chess. New York: Greenwillow, 1987. (Tote craft)

Hiser, Berniece T. *The Adventures of Charles and His Wheat-Straw Hat*. Illustrated by Mary Szilagyi. New York: Dodd, Mead, 1986. (Fiction)

Hissey, Jane. *Old Bear*. New York: Philomel, 1986. (Bear sit-up)

Kay, Helen. *The First Teddy Bear*. Illustrated by Susan Detwiler. Owings Mills, Md.: Stemmer House, 1985. (Bear sit-up)

Keats, Ezra Jack. *Jennie's Hat*. New York: Harper and Row, 1966. (Fiction)

Matthias, Catherine. *I Can Be a Police Officer*. Chicago: Children's Press, 1984.

Morris, Ann. *Hats, Hats, Hats*. Photographs by Ken Heyman. New York: Lothrop, Lee and Shepard, 1989. (Nonfiction)

Munari, Bruno. *Jimmy Has Lost His Cap. Where Can It Be?* New York: World, 1959. (Fiction)

Nodset, Joan L. *Who Took the Farmer's Hat?* Harper and Row, 1963. (Fiction)

Oz, Charles. *How Is a Crayon Made?* New York: Simon and Schuster, 1990. (Crayon)

Seuss, Dr. *The 500 Hats of Bartholomew Cubbins*. New York: Vanguard, 1938; New York: Random House, 1989. (Fiction)

_____. *The Cat in the Hat*. New York: Random House, 1957. (Fiction)

Slobodkina, Esphyr. *Caps for Sale*. New York: Harper, 1947. (Fiction)

Swift, Hildegarde Hoyt. *The Little Red Lighthouse and the Great Gray Bridge*. Illustrated by Lynd Ward. New York: HBJ, 1945. (Lighthouse craft)

Ungerer, Tomi. *The Hat*. New York: Parents, 1970. (Fiction)

Warner, Gertrude Chandler. *Houseboat Mystery*. Niles, Ill.: Whitman, 1967. (Houseboat craft)

_____. *Lighthouse Mystery*. Niles, Ill.: Whitman, 1967. (Lighthouse craft)

Wood, Joyce. *Grandmother Lucy and Her Hats*. New York: Atheneum, 1969. (Fiction)

10 Problems of Beginning Storytellers—and Solutions

Even the best storytellers can improve their performances. Often all that is needed is a self-review of a tape or video; however, the teacher can also provide needed help and direction through good coaching. Listed below are common problems and recommended activities for solving them. Remember to be positive and encouraging.

RATE OF DELIVERY

Too Fast. The student races through the story slurring words in a rush to get off the stage.

1. Have student imagine that he or she is telling the story to a person who is just learning English. The speech must be slow and the pronunciation clear for proper communication.

2. Have student pause and take a deep breath at the end of each sentence; or set the pauses in the written text and have the student take a breath or switch eye contact to a new person at the pause mark (see page 13). The student can also be coached not to give the next sentence until the teacher gives a signal to continue.

3. Have student imagine that a person is writing down everything. The speaker must speak more slowly so that the notetaker can keep up.

4. Teacher can call out "too fast," repeating the sentence at the correct pace for the performer to imitate.

Too Slow. The storyteller drags the story along until the listener loses track of the beginning of the sentence or idea.

1. Have student imagine that he or she is not "on-stage" but rather telling the story to a restless four year old. The teller must keep the child's attention.

2. Have student set pauses in the written text and practice not pausing between pause marks.

3. Have student time the story as tape recorded by the teacher at an appropriate pace. The student then works to tell the story in the same time frame. Have student record his or her version and compare it with the teacher's original.

PROJECTION

Too Soft. Student speaks too softly to be heard by the audience, or speaks in a "breathy" voice. These exercises may also keep the student from mumbling and fading at the end of a sentence. Nervousness, inexperience, and poor breathing all contribute to the problem.

1. Have student stand in a closet with the door closed or tell the story facing away from the audience. The student's goal is to be heard from the back of the room even while in the closet or with the back turned. A student coach either knocks on the door of the closet or knocks on a nearby desk if a student in the audience signals that he or she can't hear. The storyteller then knows to speak louder. When the volume seems appropriate, the door is opened and the student turns to face the audience using the same projection. If projection drops, the student returns to the closet and faces the wall again until the volume is correctly adjusted.

2. Have student imagine that the room is like a great umbrella and that his or her voice must fill the umbrella and project to all edges of the umbrella.

3. Have student imagine that the voices originates from the waistline area (diaphragm), gaining in volume and tone as it goes through the chest and out the megaphone (mouth).

4. To focus on the diaphragm, have student lie on the floor and place a book on the diaphragm (just above the waist.) Book should rise and fall as student breathes. Then have student get up and repeat the movement while standing.

Too Loud. The student's voice booms out, sometimes sounding harsh or shrill. (Very few students will have this problem.)

1. Have student observe the audience looking for nonverbal cues that the delivery is too loud, such as facial grimaces, no eye contact, or other students actually covering their ears.

2. Have student tell a story in a conversational tone to a partner. Have the listening student move away gradually. When the listening student has trouble hearing, the student touches his or her ear. As soon as the volume is appropriate, the student nods. The speaker continues to adjust the volume until the listening student reaches the back of the space.

3. Working with a microphone is tricky because each system is different. An audience can feel assaulted by a loud sound system. The speaker must practice with the system in the space where the performance will take place. Most microphones are held approximately five inches below and slightly in front of the chin. The speaker may use a conversational volume with most microphones. An assistant or teacher should stand in the back of the room signaling to the speaker to adjust the volume as necessary.

BODY IMAGE

Nervousness. The student is flushed, and the voice or hands may shake. "Butterflies" in the stomach may cause inappropriate giggling, and in extreme cases the student may not be able to talk at all. Taking in air in shallow breaths and not releasing it as frequently as normal is often a sign of nervousness.

1. The teacher should stress that nervousness is absolutely normal and may help energize the telling. The teacher may want to have all student storytellers do some warm-up activities, such as:

Vocal Warm-ups

- Breathe in and out slowly. Place your hands around your rib cage and feel how air fills your lungs and pushes out the rib cage. Repeat. Breathe in and count to ten aloud.

- Pretend your mouth is like a rubber band that stretches in this sequence: right, left, up, down, drawn in like an old person's mouth, pursed like a fish, and stretching in all directions.

2. Have students sit in their chairs and imagine that a warm, comfortable jacket has been placed on their shoulders. They should imagine that the warmth and weight of the jacket is making the tension drain out of their bodies. They should close their eyes and visualize the tension flowing away.

3. Have students visualize themselves doing an outstanding job in front of a group. Suggest that they see themselves smiling and comfortable and finally hearing the audience applaud.

4. Have students take small steps: practice telling the story out loud to themselves, then to a partner, then to a small group, and finally to the whole class.

Too Many or Distracting Gestures. The student flails the arms like a wounded sparrow, paces back and forth, or shifts from one foot to the other. The student plays with marbles in the pocket or twists a strand of hair. The listeners forget the story as they intently watch the distracting purposeless gestures.

1. The first step, of course, is to make the student aware of the gestures. The teacher can do this either by critique or through a joint viewing of a videotape.

2. Ron Hoff, in *I Can See You Naked*, suggests that one "stand in front of a full-length mirror with a large book in each hand. Then talk. At times you'll raise one hand or the other in gesture even through the books are heavy. Those are real gestures. Save them. Eliminate others. Those are nervous gestures" (Hoff 1988, 63).

3. Make sure the student removes all pocket objects and has empty hands (except for possible props) when it is time to speak.

4. If the student is a "wanderer," put an X on the floor. The student reviews the story and decides when a change in position would signal a change in the story. Often this occurs in a transition in the story such as a change in location, a new character speaking, or the passage of time. The student then marks the story with a "stage" note (e.g., take two steps left) indicating a shift in position. This should eliminate "mindless wandering."

No Gestures. The student is frozen in a rigid stance. Arms may be clasped in front or back or held stiffly at the side of the body, never moving.

1. Have the student make up a language called gibberish, composed of vowels and consonants just as in English. The student either tells the story he or she is working on (or a familiar tale such as "Little Red Riding Hood," in gibberish using voice inflections, facial expressions, and gestures to convey the meaning of the story. If the story is a familiar one, the other students can guess which story it is. The student can then retell the story in real language, using some of the gestures suggested in the gibberish exercise.

2. Write emotions (fear, happiness, disgust, confusion, anxiety, etc.) on cards. Have student show the emotion with gestures or facial expressions. The same process could be used to show action (opening a jar, slamming a door shut, blowing out a candle, etc.) The student should then analyze the story to be told and write "stage notes" as reminders of gestures and facial expressions to be used.

3. Again, the student could tell a story in front of a full-length mirror to add and analyze appropriate gestures.

4. The student could keep a gesture log analyzing gestures used by people every day or by performers on television, noting each gesture and the meaning it conveys.

5. Any of the pantomime activities suggested in chapter 1 (see pp. 7-8) could also be used.

Disparate Facial and Vocal Expressions. The student uses an angry voice with a pleasant expression or a pleasant voice with an angry expression, or other combinations of voice and face that send mixed signals.

1. Have the student practice coordinating voice and expression by using a mirror.

2. Have the student become more aware of the "story of the face" by reading faces in the newspaper or magazines before looking at the story. Have the student ask, "What is this person thinking or feeling?"

3. Ask the student to watch television with the sound off and practice reading faces.

4. Make a game out of "pass the face." A facial expression is passed from student to student changing the expression at intervals set by the teacher. Students can guess which emotion other students are conveying.

LANGUAGE

Frequent Use of Fillers. The student uses distracting phrases such as "hmm," "you know," and "like I said" as fillers during the story.

1. Have the student listen to a recording of the story as he or she presented it, and note the use of filler words. The student needs to understand the frequency of those words before they can be reduced or eliminated.

2. The student should then retell the story substituting filler words with a breath. Instruct the speaker to take a breath, hold it for a moment, and then continue the story. Although one might think that this would produce a choppy story, the pauses (breaths) in most cases seem quite natural.

Garbled Speech. The student has poor enunciation:

- Dropping the *g* in *ing*, for example,
    walkin' (walking)
    havin' (having)

- Dropping or mispronouncing the *t* or *d* in the middle of a word, for example,
    tweny (twenty)
    stard (started)

- Failing to clearly enunciate so that listeners may not be able to hear the difference between beginning consonant sounds *d/t, g/k, b/p,* for example.

- Failing to open the mouth enough to produce rounded vowel tones (a problem especially for beginners).

1. The best remedy for poor articulation is for the teacher to pronounce the word correctly and have the student repeat the correct sounds.

2. Say tongue twisters together as a class and have students overenunciate every word. Repeat the tongue twisters six times:

    selfish shellfish

    rubber baby buggy bumpers

    red leather, yellow leather

    unique New York

    toy boat

3. Ask the speech pathologist in your school to recommend exercises for practicing better articulation; or refer to exercises described in the books by Glass, Linklater, Linver, and McClosky, in the bibliography for this chapter.

STAGE PRESENCE

Memory Problems. The student is telling a story when suddenly the mind goes blank and panic sets in. This happens most often when the story has been memorized rather than learned.

1. The student who has visualized a movie of the story can simply go back to the movie. The student continues telling the story describing the scene, the characters, and the remembered action. Then, more than likely, the visual image of what happens next will reappear and the teller can continue.

2. The student can draw a filmstrip of the story, which should aid visual memory. If the characters or scenes are arranged in sequence on a surface in front of the speaker, they can then serve as memory prompters.

3. Sometimes the most difficult parts to remember in a story are the transitions. Have the student draw a story map (see chapter 1, pages 23-26) with bridges between scenes. The student may actually want to write a transitional or bridging sentence on the map. For example:

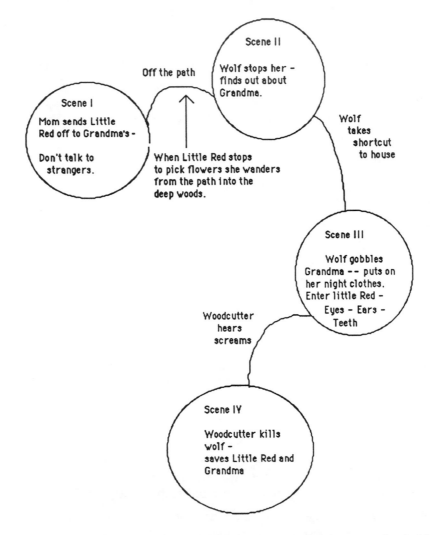

Have the students, when learning and practicing the story, concentrate on the bridges and passages. The bridges aren't as visually vivid as other scenes in the story. Mapping should help highlight the transitions.

4. The student can create a map of the story to be hung in the back of the room. The audience can't see it but the teller can. After several successful tellings the student would remove the map and simply visualize it as the story progresses.

5. For students who are chronic forgetters, the teacher may want to recommend flannel board stories. The students would arrange the characters or scenes in sequence on a surface in front of them and use the pictures as memory prompters.

Flat and Uninteresting Characters or Descriptions. As the student tells the story it is hard to distinguish one character from another. Listeners can't visualize the characters or the scenes. There is a good chance that if listeners can't visualize the characters and the scenes vividly, neither can the teller.

1. First make sure the student likes the story to be presented.

2. Have the student, working with a partner, describe how the character is dressed, how the character walks, what the character sounds like, how old and how tall the character is, etc. Although including all of this descriptive detail may be inappropriate in the story, the teller must be able to visualize the detail to bring the character to life. The same is true of the scenes in the story. The teller needs to see the scene vividly in order to make it live for the listener.

3. Have the teller draw pictures of the characters or the scenes in the story.

4. Have the student carefully observe and record details of a real person or one on television who is like a character in the story and then describe that person to a partner.

5. Sometimes description problems stem from an inadequate student vocabulary. The student who is using someone else's story should review the author's use of descriptive language. The student who is telling an original story might use a thesaurus to hunt for more vivid words or keep a word-find journal, writing down vivid words or unusually descriptive phrases read or heard. These words or phrases can be used in later stories.

Poor Eye Contact. The student tells the story to the floor, the ceiling tiles, or the side walls. Sometimes the student looks only at the teacher, avoiding eye contact with classmates.

1. Good eye contact, like other skills, must be practiced. Have the student walk around the room and say a short phrase (such as "Hi, my name is Franklin Smith and today I'm going to tell you a story about a monster called the Abominable Snowman"), looking directly into three to five listeners' eyes.

2. Next, have the student repeat the same exercise, but this time the student comes to the front of the room, stops, establishes eye contact with three people, repeats the selected phrases, says thank you, establishes eye contact with three more people, then walks off center stage.

3. Ask the students to "Zorro" the audience at each presentation, forming a big sweeping **Z** with the eyes. It isn't possible to establish eye contact with all listeners, but, this gives the audience the feeling they are being included in the story.

Lack of Fluidity. The storyteller jerks and jars through the story, pausing at inappropriate places and rushing through others.

1. This problem sometimes takes care of itself when the student becomes more familiar with the story and has practiced it aloud a number of times. If not....

2. Have the student sit in a chair and pretend to be an old man or woman telling the story to small children seated at the storyteller's feet. The teller leans forward, elbows on knees, and tells the story in a quiet voice.

3. Have the student tell the story out loud a number of times as rapidly as possible, then at the appropriate pace.

Monotone Speech. The student tells the story at one speed and with little or no voice inflection to show emotions.

1. Have the student make up a language called gibberish, composed of vowels and consonants just as in English. Using a well-known fairy tale or folktale, the student communicates the meaning of the story with voice inflection and physical language. Have a partner guess which story the teller is sharing. The student should then examine his or her own story for appropriate inflection and physical language.

2. Have the student repeat a sentence such as, "On Tuesday an eight-foot bear walked into my bedroom."

- Very quickly—to convey excitement
- Very slowly—to show disappointment
- Tentatively—to show fear
- Moderately—to state a fact

3. Have the student work with a written copy of the story, marking pauses, voice inflections, and changes in speed. A partner could then work with this "script" or an unmarked copy of the story to show how the teller actually told the story.

4. Review the exercises in chapter 1 (pages 9-13) to practice showing emotion with voice, tone, and pacing.

Sloppy or Tentative Stance. The student slouches in front of the group or hunches over, trying to look inconspicuous.

1. Have the student walk boldly to the front of the room, stop, establish eye contact with at least three other students, take a deep breath (pretending to be an opera singer), and then begin to tell the story.

2. Have the student pretend to be a puppet. The main string is attached to the head pulling the puppet up straight and tall. With the head properly positioned, the chin, shoulders, and chest fall naturally in line.

Hasty Exit. Barely has the last word been spoken when the student charges off the stage.

1. When the tale is finished, have the student say a final line such as, "And that's the story of how the giraffe got its spots" (letting the voice drop on the last word), count to three silently, say thank you, and then leave the stage.

STORY LENGTH

Improper Length. The story either goes on and on or is unsatisfyingly short.

1. Some students, particularly young students, have difficulty distinguishing between important and unimportant detail. The teacher should review the story with each child and assist with the editing before the student begins to develop the tale for oral telling.

2. The original story can be recorded on audio tape, listened to, then retold into the tape recorder from memory. The student can then compare the original version to the second recording. Sometimes the brain does an excellent job of editing out the unimportant detail.

3. If the student has shortened the story too much, the teacher can help the student reanalyze the tale, reinserting material that will make the story come alive.

CONCLUSION

Working with students on the problems discussed in this chapter will certainly add polish to the performance; however, remember that storytelling is to be enjoyed. Let the children experience the joy and excitement of telling and listening before you begin to help them perfect their performance.

BIBLIOGRAPHY

Glass, Lillian. *Talk to Win*. New York: Putnam, 1987.

Hoff, Ron. *I Can See You Naked*. New York: Andrews and McMeel, 1988.

Linklater, Kristin. *Freeing the Natural Voice*. New York: Drama Book Publishers, 1976.

Linver, Sandy. *Speak Easy: How to Talk Your Way to the Top*. New York: Summit Books, 1978.

McClosky, David Blair. *Your Voice at Its Best*. Rev. ed. Boston: Boston Music Company, 1978.

McClosky, David Blair, and Barbara H. McClosky. *Voice in Song and Speech*. Boston: Boston Music Company, 1984.

Osgood, Charles. *Osgood on Speaking*. New York: William Moore and Company, 1988.

Additional Resources

CREATIVE DRAMATICS/THEATRE

Alexander, Robert. *Improvisational Theatre for the Classroom*. Edited by Wendy Haynes. Washington, D.C.: Living Stage Theatre Company for the U.S. Department of Education, 1983.

Hennings, Dorothy Grant. *Smiles, Nods and Pauses*. New York: Citation, 1974.

Hodgson, John, and Ernest Richards. *Improvisation*. New York: Grove, 1979.

McCaslin, Nellie. *Creative Drama in the Classroom*. 4th ed. New York and London: Longman, 1984.

Novelly, Marcia. *Theatre Games for Young Performers*. Colorado Springs, Colo.: Meriwether, 1985.

Way, Brian. *Development through Drama*. Atlantic Highlands, N.J.: Humanities, 1986.

FOLKLORE

Arthur, Stephen, and Julia Arthur. *Your Life & Times: How to Put a Life Story on Tape—An Oral History Handbook*. Nobleton, Fla.: Heritage Tree, 1986.

Bosma, Bette. *Fairy Tales, Fables, Legends, and Myths*. New York: Teachers College Press, 1987.

Handbook of American Folklore. Edited by Richard M. Dorson. Bloomington: Indiana University Press, 1986.

Wigginton, Eliot. *Sometimes a Shining Moment: The Foxfire Experience*. Garden City, N.Y.: Anchor, 1986.

Zeitlin, Steven J., Amy J. Kotkin, and Holly Cutting Baker. *A Celebration of American Family Folklore*. New York: Pantheon, 1982.

STORYTELLING

Baker, August, and Ellin Greene. *Storytelling: Art and Technique*. New York and London: Bowker, 1977.

Barton, Bob. *Tell Me Another*. Markham, Ont.: Pembroke, 1986.

Bauer, Caroline Feller. *Handbook for Storytellers*. Chicago: American Library Association, 1977.

_____. *This Way to Books*. New York: Wilson, 1983.

Breneman, Lucille N., and Bren Breneman. *Once Upon a Time*. Chicago: Nelson-Hall, 1983.

Briggs, Nancy E., and Joseph A. Wagner. *Children's Literature through Storytelling and Drama*. 2d ed. Dubuque: Brown, 1979.

Butler, Francelia. *Sharing Literature with Children*. New York and London: Longman, 1977.

Dailey, Sheila. *Storytelling: A Creative Teaching Strategy*. Mt. Pleasant, Mich.: Author, 1985.

DeWitt, Dorothy. *Children's Faces Looking Up*. Chicago: American Library Association, 1979.

Geisler, Harlynne. *The Best of the Story Bag*. San Diego: Harlynne Geisler, 1988.

Greene, Ellin, and George Shannon. *Storytelling: A Selected Annotated Bibliography*. New York and London: Garland, 1986.

Griffin, Barbara Budge. *Students as Storytellers: The Long and the Short of Learning a Story*. 4th ed. Medford, Oreg.: Barbara Budge Griffin, 1989.

Hamilton, Martha, and Mitch Weiss. *Children Tell Stories: A Guide for Teachers*. Ithaca, N.Y.: Tandem, 1988.

Livo, Norma J., and Sandra A. Rietz. *Storytelling Activities*. Littleton, Colo.: Libraries Unlimited, 1987.

_____. *Storytelling: Process and Practice*. Littleton, Colo.: Libraries Unlimited, 1986.

Pellowski, Anne. *The Family Storytelling Handbook*. London and New York: Macmillan, 1987.

_____. *The World of Storytelling*. New York and London: Bowker, 1977.

Peterson, Carolyn Sue, and Brenny Hall. *Story Programs: A Source Book of Materials*. Metuchen, N.J. and London: Scarecrow, 1980.

Ross, Ramon. *Storyteller*. 2d ed. Columbus, Toronto, London, and Sydney: Merrill, 1972.

Sawyer, Ruth. *The Way of the Storyteller*. New York: Penguin, 1984.

Schimmel, Nancy. *Just Enough to Make a Story: A Sourcebook for Storytelling*. 2d ed. Berkeley, Calif.: Sisters' Choice Press, 1982.

Shenkman, Richard. *Legends, Lies, and Cherished Myths of American History*. New York: Harper and Row, 1988.

Wilson, Jane B. *The Story Experience*. Metuchen, N.J. and London: Scarecrow, 1979.

Ziskind, Sylvia. *Telling Stories to Children*. New York: Wilson, 1976.

Index

About the Authors

Harriet R. Kinghorn holds the degree of Bachelor of Science in Education from the University of Nebraska, Lincoln, and the Master of Science in Education from the University of North Dakota. She has taught preschool, kindergarten, and grades two through four. Harriet is presently teaching enrichment classes in the elementary schools in East Grand Forks, Minnesota. She has authored and coauthored articles in national educational magazines as well as numerous activity books including *At Day's End* (a book of themes for independent learning in grades three through six) published by Libraries Unlimited, 1988. Harriet was recognized as one of twelve "Honor Teachers of Minnesota" in 1976.

Mary Helen Pelton holds a doctorate in education from the University of Denver. She has been a classroom teacher in Colorado, Minnesota, and Maine; a district superintendent of schools in Maine; and is the assistant dean of the Division of Continuing Education at the University of North Dakota. She teaches graduate courses at the University of North Dakota in storytelling, use of oral language, and reading. Mary Helen has performed professionally as a storyteller since 1983. She is a popular presenter at local, regional, and national conferences and institutes.